AF255214

Saadia Gaon, The Earliest Hebrew Grammarian

Saadia Gaon, The Earliest Hebrew Grammarian

By

SOLOMON L. SKOSS

*Late Professor of Arabic at The Dropsie College
for Hebrew and Cognate Learning*

WIPF & STOCK · Eugene, Oregon

Wipf and Stock Publishers
199 W 8th Ave, Suite 3
Eugene, OR 97401

Saadia Gaon, The Earliest Hebrew Grammarian
By Skoss, Solomon L.
Softcover ISBN-13: 978-1-6667-6691-2
Hardcover ISBN-13: 978-1-6667-6692-9
eBook ISBN-13: 978-1-6667-6693-6
Publication date 12/5/2022
Previously published by Dropsie College Press, 1955

Dedicated to my Wife

IRENE SKOSS

a woman of valour

אֵשֶׁת־חַיִל מִי יִמְצָא

וְרָחֹק מִפְּנִינִים מִכְרָהּ

"A woman of valour who can find?
For her price is far above rubies."
(Proverbs 31.10)

FOREWORD

by Abraham A. Neuman
President, The Dropsie College

This treatise on *Saadia Gaon, the Earliest Hebrew Grammarian*, appeared originally in serial form in the *Proceedings of the American Academy for Jewish Research* (Volumes XXI, XXII and XXIII). These studies were the last gleanings of a rich and ripe life devoted sacrificially to research and scholarship. That these studies are now secured in book form is due wholly to the devotion of Mrs. Irene Skoss, the wife of the sainted author, Solomon L. Skoss ע״ה, and to the generosity of her brother, James S. Kapnek. Hebrew and Semitic scholars throughout the world will be grateful for this intellectual gift.

Solomon L. Skoss, a descendant of a long line of rabbis and scholars, was born at Chusovaya, in the Province of Perm, Russia, in 1884. He came to this country in 1907, subsequently entered the University of Denver and there obtained the B.A. and M.A. degrees.

His interests at the University of Denver were centered in science. In pursuance of these studies, he came to Philadelphia for advanced work in apiology. Before long, however, he found his way to the Dropsie College where he devoted himself to Arabic and general Semitic studies. After two years, he was granted a leave of absence and he proceeded to Cairo, Egypt, where he studied at the Egyptian University and the School of Oriental Studies of the American University of Cairo. On his return from Egypt, he received the degree of Doctor of Philosophy from the Dropsie College and was appointed at his Alma Mater to fill the vacancy created by the untimely death of Professor Ben Zion Halper.

The rapidity with which Doctor Skoss mastered all aspects of Arabic studies, classical and Judeo-Arabic, is an index of his fertile mind and his intense zeal. In a relatively short period, he gained recognition as one of the foremost authorities in Judeo-Arabic and in Karaitica. In addition to numerous articles in learned journals, he published two major works: *The Arabic Commentary of Ali ben Suleiman on Genesis* (Philadelphia, 1928), and the *Hebrew-Arabic Dictionary of the Bible of David ben Abraham al-Fasi* (2 volumes, New Haven, 1936–1942).

One of his keenest delights and scientific achievements lay in bringing to light and identifying ancient and long vanished fragments of Judaic literature. Despite a serious heart ailment from which he suffered many years, he undertook long and laborious trips to world-famous libraries, i. e., the Asiatic Museum in Leningrad in 1932, the Cambridge and Oxford libraries in England in 1948 and 1952, in order to search for vanished fragments of Jewish and Karaite writings. Upon the invitation of his former student, Professor Abraham I. Katsh, he traveled to Israel to teach his favorite subject at the Berl Katznelson Institute of Social Science during the summer of 1950. To Doctor Skoss and his wife, this was a spiritual pilgrimage.

It was altogether fitting that the twilight period of his creative life should be devoted to Saadiana, and especially to the grammatical and lexical work of Saadia Gaon, which was destined to serve as a vehicle for and a stimulus to the established scientific achievements of the Spanish school.

Saadia's studies were consciously directed to an appeal to foster the holy tongue "which our God has chosen of old"; to put an end to "the distorting of our tongue in our captivity"; to use it creatively, to let it "ring among us all." Working so assiduously to bring to light Saadia's illumination of the Hebrew tongue in all its nuances was in the case of Doctor Skoss an act of self-revelation, in which he expressed his own profound love of the holy tongue and the satisfying joy of direct contact with the rich and varied heritage hidden in Jewish Arabic letters.

As a colleague and friend of many years, I cannot conclude this Foreword without a brief word about the man whom all of us, students and colleagues alike, admired and loved. Great as was the scholar, greater still were the noble attributes of his character and personality. He was essentially a man of peace who truly loved his fellowmen. He was self-sacrificing, meek and humble, fulfilling in letter and spirit the prophet's mandate: to do justly, to love mercy and to walk humbly with God.

Philadelphia
March 1, 1955

CONTENTS

Saadia Gaon, The Earliest Hebrew Grammarian

SAADIA GAON, THE EARLIEST HEBREW GRAMMARIAN

INTRODUCTION

Abraham ibn Ezra, in his Introduction to *Moznayim*, presents a list of early Hebrew philologists, or זקני לשון הקדש, as he terms them, and at the head of the list is R. Saadia Gaon, to whom he refers as ראש המדברים בכל מקום. Indeed, he was the first who wrote in Arabic a separate work entirely devoted to the study of the grammar of the Hebrew language. This work inaugurates the study of Hebrew grammar as a separate discipline, entirely independent of masoretic studies, to which it was previously appended, as, e. g., *Diqduqe ha-Ṭeʻamim* of the masorete Aaron ben Asher, against whom Saadia wrote a polemical work, according to Dunash b. Labraṭ.[1]

This earliest Hebrew grammar is referred to by its author by the full Arabic title כתאב פציח לגֿה אלעבראניין[2] (Book of Elegance of the Language of the Hebrews), but more often he calls it by the short title כתב אללגֿה[3] (Books on the [Hebrew] Language), or simply אלי"ב גֿז[4] (The Twelve Parts), of which this work consists. Dunash, the earliest authority referring to this work by name beside Saadia himself, calls it in Hebrew כתב צחות לשון, כתב צחות לשון הקדש, ספר צחות לשון הקדש

---

[1] *Teshubot* against Saadia, No. 72; see the writer's "A Study of Hebrew Vowels" etc., *JQR*, N. S., XLII, 287, and n. 22, *ad loc.*

[2] *Ibid.*, 290, 2.

[3] *Commentaire sur le Séfer Yesira*, 75, 21; 76, 4.

[4] Beginning of Part III, *JQR*, N. S., XXXIII, 174, 1 (*Saadia Studies*, Philadelphia, 1943, 66, 1); *Sefer ha-Galuy*, ed. Harkavy, in *Studien u. Mittheil.*, V, 157, 11.

העברי, or simply כתב צחות הלשון,[5] where צחות, the Arabic פציח, was evidently intended to mean grammatical correctness of speech.[6] Ibn Janāḥ refers to this work as כתאב אללגה,[7] rendered by Ibn Tibbon ספר חכמת הלשון,[8] while Abraham ibn Ezra, who most likely learned of it from the criticism of Dunash, thought that it comprised two treatises which he calls ספר לשון עברית and ספר צחות.[9]

Until recently the only information we had of this first attempt at independent treatment of Hebrew grammar was the quotations from it by Saadia himself in his Commentary on *Sefer Yeṣirah*[10] and in the criticism (תשובות) of the Gaon's views by R. Mebasser (or Mubashshir)[11] and by Dunash, as well as in the rejoinder to the latter by Abraham ibn Ezra in שפת יתר. A few grammatical points are likewise to be found in Saadia's Introduction to the Agron[12] and in his biblical commentaries so far published. This rather scanty material was carefully studied by Bacher and fully utilized in his presentation of Saadia's grammatical views in *Anfänge der hebräischen Grammatik*, which appeared in *ZDMG* of 1895.[13] It is really quite amazing how much information, though not always correct, Bacher was able to glean from the very scanty material at his disposal.

However, just one year after Bacher's study was published, Harkavy identified in the Second Firkovitch Collection at the Leningrad Public Library some extensive fragments of Saadia's grammatical work "Kutub al-Lughah" itself.[14] Several years ago

---

[5] *Teshubot*, Nos. 98, 102, 104, 120.
[6] Bacher, *Anfänge d. hebr. Grammatik*, 39.
[7] *Kitāb al-Lumaʿ*, 3, 22 f.
[8] *Riqmah*, 12, 7.
[9] Introduction to *Moznayim*.
[10] *Commentaire*, 45, 5 ff.; 75, 6 ff.; 76, 2 ff., to 79, 14.
[11] Harkavy, *op. cit.*, 68 ff.; 182 ff.; Malter, *Saadia Gaon*, 50, n. 82, 324.
[12] Edited by Harkavy in *op. cit.*, 39 ff.
[13] Pp. 38–62.
[14] In the letters of Harkavy to Poznański, edited by Assaf in זכרון לאחרונים,

I secured photostats of this Leningrad Ms., consisting of 55 leaves, and of an 8-leaf fragment of his *Agron*.[15] During the summer of 1948 I was fortunate enough to identify at the Bodleian Library in Oxford and in the Taylor-Schechter Genizah Collection at Cambridge University Library four additional fragments of this Grammar, which fill in part some lacunae in the Leningrad fragments.[16] So we can at present gain a pretty fair idea of the Gaon's views on Hebrew grammar.

The fragments so far identified embrace portions of the following parts:

Part II. A Study of Augmentation and Contraction (or Amplification and Elision) in Hebrew Stems.

Part III. A Study of Inflection of Particles, Nouns, and Verbs.

Part IV. Rules of Dagesh and Rafe.

Part V. A Study of the Vowels, the places in the mouth where they originate, and their combination and interchange with each other.

Part VI. A Study of the Shewa.

Part VII. A Study of Laryngeal and non-Laryngeal letters with regard to the vocalization of servile letters which are added to them.

Part VIII. A Study of Laryngeals and the changes that take place in their vocalization as compared with non-Laryngeals.

Finally, there are a few leaves probably belonging to Part IX, treating of Expletives and Affixes and their usage under various conditions.

Jerusalem, 1936, No. 8, Harkavy mentions that he identified the fragments of "Kutub al-Lughah," more than 40 leaves, on March 3rd, 1896, but at present these fragments comprise 55 leaves; see also Nos. 11, 13 (about the *Agron*), 26, 27, and 64.

[15] See my report in *JQR*, N. S., XXIII, 329 ff.

[16] For a brief report see Year Book of American Philosophical Society, 1948, 211 ff.

by him from כתאב אצול אלשער, which evidently was an enlarged
version of the *Agron*, this material was more than likely also
included in the first part of "Kutub al-Lughah", since the ques-
tion of which combinations of consonants do not occur in Hebrew
was discussed there at length. For the same reason the combination of consonants כע, כץ, לר, נל, סז, marked in the Leningrad fragment of the *Agron* with לא נמצא,[23] were probably
likewise included in that part. Moreover, we may similarly
assume that Menaḥem's extensive list of consonants not com-
bining with each other[24] is primarily based on material of the
first part of Saadia's Grammar, though the former omits the
combinations of יו, יי, יך, כע, עך, given by the Gaon, as pointed
out recently by Allony.[25]

But apart from the above-mentioned matter pertaining to
the letters of the alphabet, which was treated in the first part,
Dunash b. Labraṭ also mentions that Saadia divided the 22
letters into two groups of eleven each: those used as servile
letters and those that could be radicals only. The latter made
for them mnemonic sentences: איתן בשלום כה for the eleven
servile letters and טח ספר גזע צדק for the eleven radicals. But
Dunash points out that ד and ט should likewise be included
among the servile letters, for they replace the ת in *hitpa'el* after
ז and צ respectively, as הזדמנתון (Dan. 2.9 *qere*), נצטדק (Gen.
44.16). Accordingly, he offers the mnemonic sentences אדניה
שלו כתם טב for the thirteen servile letters and חג קץ ספר עז for
the nine radicals.[26] Now there is good reason to believe that,
in his criticism of Saadia, Dunash refers to the first part of
"Kutub al-Lughah" and not to his *Agron*, for in the Hebrew
Introduction to the latter the mnemonic words for servile letters

---

[23] *Ha-Goren*, VI (1906), 26, n. 1.   [24] *Maḥberet*, 10b.
[25] *Tarbiz*, XIX (1948), 103.
[26] *Teshubot*, No. 6; see Ibn Janāḥ's criticism in *Luma'*, 35, 25 ff. (*Mustalḥaq*,
130 ff.), and Ibn Ezra, *Sefat Yeter*, No. 6, and *Ṣaḥot*, 17a and 25a.

are האובים כשתלן,[27] not mentioned by Dunash. Seven of these, בשלום כה, are prefixed both to nouns and to verbs, while the remaining four, איתן, are prefixed to verbs only. But in Part VII of this Grammar, where both the servile and the radical letters are mentioned, the former are given in aphabetical order: אבהו יכל מנשת, while the latter have the afore-mentioned mnemonic sentence. The same arrangement of the servile letters prefixed to a word is found likewise in a fragment of Saadia's Commentary on Ex. 25.33–5, published by Harkavy, where they are compared to the eleven ornamental knobs of the candlestick in the Tabernacle.[28]

Thus, Part One of "Kutub al-Lughah" must have embraced the following subject matter: (a) A study of the 22 letters of the alphabet; (b) Their division into the five organs of speech: laryngeals, palatals, linguals, dentals, and labials; (c) Which of the letters can, or cannot, join with each other in one word, and (d) Their division into eleven servile and eleven radical letters, with the mnemonic sentences איתן בשלום כה for the former and טח ספר גזע צדק for the latter.

II. Augmentation and Contraction

In the second part of his Grammar Saadia deals with Augmentation and Contraction, or Amplification and Elision, in Hebrew stems (אלקול פי אלתפכים ואלאכתצאר). He explains the doubling of consonants in geminate verbs, as well as the *pi'lel* forms of ע"ו and ע"י verbs (as קומם, התבונן), by augmentation (אלתפכים), for their stems are, in his opinion, primarily bi-consonantal. So he considers ותוללינו (Ps. 137.3) an augmented form of תלינו (ibid. 2), rendered by him מעלקונא[29] and עלקנא respectively, or ארומם (Isa. 33.10) is an augmented form of

---

[27] Harkavy, *op. cit.*, 57, 11 ff.

[28] *Ibid.*, 20, n. 6, and 59, n. 65.　　[29] So also *Jāmi' al-Alfāẓ*, II, 735, 31 f.

אָרוֹם (Ps. 46.11), etc. Saadia cites one or more instances of such augmentations of every letter of the alphabet. The fragment of the Leningrad Ms. containing this part begins here with letter *lamed.*

Moreover, formations of *pilpel* verbs are likewise considered by Saadia augmented forms, for their stems are bi-consonantal. So סַלְסְלֶהָ (Prov. 4.8) is an augmented form of סַלּוּ (Isa. 62.10) and ערער תתערער (Jer. 51.58) are augmented from עֲרֶה (Zeph. 2.14). This applies also to forms like בחלקלקות (Dan. 11.21), which means the same as בחלקות (ibid. 32). But such gemination of two consonants occurs, in his opinion, only in transitive, not in intransitive verbs. Accordingly, not every stem may be augmented by gemination of its two consonants, and one cannot form, e. g., דברבר from דבר or שמעמע from שמע, etc. He does not mention, however, constructions like אדמדם (Lev. 13.42), שחרחרת (Cant. 1.6), formed from the intransitive stems אדם and שחר, respectively.[30]

The second subject treated in this part is contraction in Hebrew stems (אלאכתצאר), or elision of a consonant in them. Saadia discusses various types of contration or elision, such as occur in words without pronominal affixes, as the *alef* in שְׁרֵית (1 Chron. 12.38 (39))=שארית; קרְים (Ps. 99.6 *qere*)=קראים; חֹטְים (1 Sam. 14.33 *qere*)=חטאים; הַבֵּרלתָי (1 Chron. 11.39)= הַבְּאֵרלתָי (2 Sam. 23.37). The contraction in these and similar instances, which are without pronominal affixes, is inherent in them and quite natural in such words.[31]

Elision in verbs with pronominal affixes occurs either when the elided consonant is adjacent to the affix or not adjacent to it.

---

[30] The use of תפכים by David b. Abraham and of פיאור, its Hebrew equivalent, by Dunash (*Teshubot*, No. 110) is discussed later in the part treating of Expletives and Affixes.

[31] Cf. *Jāmiʿ al-Alfāẓ*, I, 18, 31 ff. Some of these forms, as שרית, ותזרני (2 Sam. 22.40), etc., are considered defective (אלנואקץ) by David b. Abraham, see *Jāmiʿ*, II, 727, 14 ff.

Instances of the former are as, e. g., אכל bеcomes לֹא אָכָל (Gen. 24.33), הביא—אלך and השיב become אביא and אשיב, respectively. Following the theory that the *maṣdar*, or verbal noun, precedes the action or condition which is expressed by the finite verb that is derived from it, an opinion maintained also by most Arab grammarians,[32] Saadia considers nominal forms like מסע, מקרא, מחנה, מראה, as stems of תחנה, אראה (Ps. 27.8), יקרא, and ויסע, respectively, with the *mem* elided in them.[33] As in the case of augmentation, Saadia emphasizes here, too, that such elisions take place only in intransitive verbs. But in verbs like יַהֲרֹג (Isa. 14.30), יִּהְדֹּף[34] (Prov. 10.3) the *he* is not elided because they are transitive.

Instances of elision of a consonant not adjacent to the affix, cited by Saadia, comprise largely the omission of the *he* in *waw* consecutive forms of ל"ה verbs. So וַיֵּרָא (Ps. 18.11) — ידאה (Deut. 28.49); וַתֵּלָא (Job 4.5) — תלאה (ibid. 2); וָאֵרָא (Gen. 31.10) — ואראה (Gen. 18.21); גֵּא (Isa. 16.6) — גֵּאֶה (Jer. 48.29), etc. He cites instances of such elisions after every letter of the alphabet.

At the end of this part Saadia appended, at the request of a student of the Hebrew language, a brief survey of the formation of tenses of the Hebrew verb, but it really belongs to Part III which treats of Inflection in Hebrew. Since it gives a general idea of Saadia's views about some important aspects of the verb, I shall present it here briefly.

---

[32] See *Mufaṣṣal²*, 16, 10 f., Wright, *Arabic Grammar³*, I, 110 B.

[33] This applies also to nominal forms like תודה, תנובה, that they are, in Saadia's opinion, the stems (אצול) of their finite verbs אודה (Gen. 29.35), ינובון (Ps. 92.15), respectively, with the *taw* elided in them.

[34] Saadia's view that the *he* in הדף is a radical and not an "added" consonant is criticized by Menaḥem (*Maḥberet*, 68b f.) who associates הדף with ודף (Lev. 26.36) and דפי (Ps. 50.20); see also *Maḥberet*, s. v. דף. The latter opinion is maintained likewise by David b. Abraham, see *Jāmi' al-Alfāẓ*, I, 399, 12 ff., 425, 24 f., where it is stated that the *he* in להדף (Deut. 6.19) is added (לאחקה), its stem being the same as in ידפנו (Job 32.14).

He takes the 3rd per. masc. sing. of the past tense (or the perfect) as the form from which the formation of the present and future tenses (or the active participle and the imperfect) could be deduced. Then he proceeds to discuss the various forms of the past tense in accordance with the number of consonants it consists of: two, three, four, or more.[35] So in bi-consonantal verbs the 3rd per. masc. sing. of the past and the present are alike, and they could be distinguished from each other only from the context, as, e. g., צם in the past is ואהי צם (Nehem. 1.4) in the present and אצום in the future, etc.

When the past is tri-consonantal, the tenses are formed in four ways: (1) If the first consonant is a *nun*, it is dropped in the future, as נתן, נותן, יתן; נדר, נודר, ידר, etc. (2) If the 2nd consonant of the past has a *dagesh*, a *mem* is added to its present, as יציל, מציל, הציל; יכה, מכה, הכה; ישבר, משבר, שׁבּר,[36] etc. (3) If the 2nd consonant of the past is one of the laryngeals א ה ח ע and its form is such that this consonant, were it not a laryngeal, would require a *dagesh*, then a *mem* is likewise added to its present, as יבער, מבער, בער; ימהר, ממהר, מהר, etc. (4) This section embraces the rest of tri-consonantal verbs not included in the preceding three sections. Their past, present, and future tenses are formed in the following manner: בוחר; בחר, יבחר; אמר, אומר ,יאמר; בנה, בונה, יבנה; קרא, קורא, יקרא; יצא,

---

[35] Uni-consonantal stems, as discussed by David b. Abraham (*Jāmi'*, I, 5, 113 ff.), Menaḥem (*Maḥberet*, 40a ff.), and Dunash (*Teshubot* against Menaḥem 26, 27, 55),— are not mentioned by Saadia in the fragments so far identified. In fact, הכה, the stem of which is the *kaf* only, according to David, Menaḥem (*Maḥberet*, 40b, 103b), and Dunash, is considered by Saadia tri-consonantal, alongside with שבר, הציל, etc., the *he* being its first radical which is replaced by a *mem* in the participle. This appears to be the earlier stage in the development of the theory of Hebrew stems, followed by the theory of uni-consonantal stems of the above mentioned authorities. But none of them had any idea of assimilation of one consonant to another.

[36] Saadia includes הציל here among the tri-consonantal stems, evidently because of the *dagesh*, analogous to שבר, but הביא, השיב are later included by him among the quadriliterals, alongside with כלכל.

יֵצֵא, יֵצֵא, etc; except יכול and חפץ, whose past and present are alike and could be distinguished from each other only from the context.

When the past is quadriliteral, a *mem* is added to its present, as משיב, השיב; יביא, מביא, הביא; also יכלכל, מכלכל, כלכל, ישיב, etc. Similar is the case when the past has more than four consonants, as יקשיב, מקשיב, הקשיב; ישבית, משבית, השבית; or when a *taw* is added to it, as יתחזק, מתחזק, התחזק, and, moreover, when the past has six consonants, a *mem* is added to its present, as ישתולל, משתולל, השתולל, etc.

Saadia's aim in the foregoing study obviously was practical: to indicate somehow the method of forming the active participle and the imperfect (or the present and future tenses, as he refers to them) from the perfect (or past tense). Rudimentary as it is, we must not lose sight of the fact that the definite principles of the tri-consonantal theory of Hebrew stems were established by Judah Ḥayyūj more than half a century after the Gaon's death.

III. INFLECTION

In the third part of his Grammar Saadia treats of the inflection (אלתצריף) of particles, nouns, and verbs. Following the Arab grammarians, Saadia classifies language in the three usual classes: nouns, verbs, and particles. He defines them in the following terms. The noun is an expression denoting something that exists, whether a substance, as נֶטַע, זֶרַע, or an accident, as דָּבָר, אָמָר, but it has no temporal idea implied in it. The verb is a part of speech denoting an accident with the idea of time expressed in it, as אמרתי, דברתי, which denote accidents or actions, but also indicate, by the addition of afformatives, that they are in the past tense; without the latter (as אמר, דבר) there would be no indication of the tense. The particle is an expression which does not denote anything that exists nor does

it convey any full meaning when it stands by itself, as עַל, מִן,
כִי, until it is added to a word of the two above-mentioned
classes, as מִן־הַבָּקֶר (Ex. 18.13), כִי רָאִיתִי (Gen. 31.12).
Saadia divides then the eleven servile letters into two
groups, seven — ש מ ל כ ו ה ב — do not change the vocalization (אעראב)[37] of the noun to which it is prefixed, as בדבר
ודבר, הדבר, etc., where the vocalization of דבר remained unchanged. The other four prefixes — ת נ י א — change its vocalization, as תדבר, נדבר, ידבר, אֲדַבֵּר, where the vowels of דָּבָר
changed to *patah* and *sere* with a *dagesh* in the middle radical,
as it became a finite verb.

This is followed by a study of the possessive affixes, which
Saadia calls *the ten possessors* (עֶשֶׂר דּוּאָת, rendered by Abraham
ibn Ezra עֶשֶׂרת הקונים).[38] They are arranged in the following
order: 1st per. sing. and pl., 2nd per. masc. and fem. sing. and
pl., and 3rd per. masc. and fem. sing. and pl., as דברנו, דברי,
דברן, דברם, דברה, דברו, דברכן, דברכם, דבֵרֵךְ, דבֵרֵךְ. Saadia
distinguishes three tenses: *past*, *present*, and *future*. So when a
noun is changed as to become a verb, it must necessarily be
either in the *past*, as דברתי, אמרתי, or in the *future*, as אֹמַר,
אדבר, or in the *present*, as דְּבָרִי, אָמְרִי, (cf. אם אמרי Job 9.27,
מדי דברי Jer. 31.20(19)). It is quite interesting to note that
Saadia takes here the verbal noun, or the *masdar*, with pronominal suffixes, as the present tense and not the active participle, as
used by himself in the previous discussion of the formation of
tenses and likewise in late Hebrew and by Ben Asher.[39]

---

[37] On the use of the term אעראב by Saadia in the meaning of vocalization
of a grammatical form see *JQR*, N. S., XXXIII, 177, n. 8 (*Saadia Studies*,
69, n. 8).

[38] *Sahot*, 32b: ורב סעדיה הגאון יקראם עשרת הקונים, והטעם כי הם קונים
כל הדברים. See also *Safah Berurah*, 3a, and *Yesod Diqduq* in *Abraham
ibn Ezra als Grammatiker*, 12, n. 56; 108, n. 2. Cf. *Diqduqe ha-Te'amim*, 35,
n. e, and *Anfänge*, 53.

[39] *Diq. ha-Te'am.*, 35: ותאמר על הזמן הנצב דבר דברת דברים.

Now the three parts of speech vary in their degree of being inflectional. The least inflectional among them are the particles, for they take only the seven prefixes ב ה ו כ ל מ ש, as הכי, ורק, שגם, etc. The Scriptures may not have instances of every particle with all these prefixes, but the accepted usage permits it. They do not take objective suffixes, with the exception of a few of them, as, e. g., עַל, עַד, which are inflected: עָלַי, עדי, etc., nor do they have any tenses.

More inflectional are the nouns. They are divided into substances, or names of bodies, and accidents, or names of actions. Substances, in turn, fall into two groups, names of articulate beings (אשכאץ אלנאטקין), as יצחק, אברהם, which, like particles, take only the seven prefixes, as האדם, באדם, etc., but do not take any possessive suffixes, nor do they have any tenses;[39a] thus they are less inflectional than some of the particles. Names of inarticulate bodies (אסמא גיר אלנאטקין מן אלאשכאץ) take, in addition to the seven prefixes, also possessive suffixes, as ארץ— ארצי, ארצנו, etc.; עיר — עירי, עירנו, etc. Accidents, or names of actions, as חֵפֶץ, שֵׁמַע, take the seven prefixes the same as articulate and inarticulate substances, as well as the ten possessive suffixes, as חפצנו, חפצי, etc., similar to inarticulate substances, but in addition, they also take the other four prefixes ת נ י א, as תחפץ, נחפץ, יחפץ, אחפץ. Furthermore, accidents can be likewise changed into tense-forms: the past — שמעתי, the present — שֹׁמֵעִי, and the future — אשמע. However, when accidents, or verbal nouns, are changed into such tense-forms,

---

[39a] Cf. *Teshubot*, No. 104, where Saadia is quoted as stating that שמות החיים לא תקרא ולא תלוה ולא תסמך, i. e. names of articulate beings (proper nouns) do not take the article (*he*), neither the construct state, nor pronominal suffixes. But here Saadia states that these nouns take the 7 prefixes, which include the *he*. Most likely Dunash cites from portions of this part, or of other parts, so far missing in our fragments. See *Anfänge*, 55 f., and *Abraham ibn Ezra als Grammatiker*, 73, n. 11.

they cease to be termed nouns and assume the designation of verbs.

More inflectional than either the particles or the nouns are the verbs, but their inflection is in a different manner. Thus, of the seven prefixes, mentioned above, they take only three: ש ו ה, as שָׁשָׁמַעְתִּי, וְשָׁמַעְתִּי, הֲשָׁמַעְתִּי, but not the other four, for one cannot say כְּשמעתי, בשמעתי, etc.⁴⁰ Nor is it proper to state that verbs take the ten affixed personal pronouns, for it is only by the addition of these affixes that they become verbs, and without them they would be verbal nouns. However, they are more inflectional because they take beside the ten affixed personal pronouns also objective suffixes. So שמעתי may be changed to שְׁמַעְתָּיךְ by adding the objective suffix of the 2nd per. masc. sing. to the afformative of the 1st per. sing. But, in addition, the verb could be changed to a causative form, as הִשְׁמַעְתָּיךְ, where the afformative indicates the agent acting upon the person alluded to by the objective suffix, who, in turn, is acting upon the thing heard.

Accordingly, Saadia divides words into five kinds: (1) Those that have the potentiality of one indication (or modification), as ואברהם. (2) Words with the potentiality of two indications, as בקולי. (3) Words with the potentiality of three indications, as ועשיתי, for it has also a tempral allusion. (4) Words with the potentiality of four indications, as וַעֲזַרְתָּיךְ, for, in addition to the tense, it refers to two persons. (5) Words with the potentiality of five indications, as וְהַאֲכַלְתָּיךְ (Isa. 58.14), for, beside the tense, it refers to the transitive actions of two persons. Particles are not mentioned in this classification probably because they may be included either in the first or in the second group if they take pronominal suffixes.

With his peculiar predilection for computations and numbers,

---

⁴⁰ See criticism of Dunash, *Teshubot*, Nos. 114 and 124.

Saadia proceeds here to compute the numbers of forms that could be made in each of these groups. So proper nouns which take only the seven prefixes ש מ ל כ ו ה ב may be changed to 13 forms, including the addition of the *waw* to the six other prefixes, as וביעקב. Common nouns would thus have 26 forms for the sing. and the pl., but since they also take the ten possessive suffixes in both numbers, as ביתי and בָּתַּי, the number of their forms would then reach 260. In the same manner he computes the number of verbal forms of the conjugation שמע in *qal* and *hif'il* in the past and the future (perfect and imperfect), the latter including also the imperative;[41] these simple forms (אלבסאיט) are 48 in number.[42] Then follows a complete table of this conjugation in *qal* and *hif'il* with all their objective suffixes (אלמזאוגאת, אלמרכּבאת), systematically arranged, comprising 368 formations, and with the 48 simple forms their number reaches 416.

But not all simple forms take each of the ten objective suffixes; so, e. g., 1st per. sing. and pl. do not take the objective suffix of the 1st per. As Saadia puts it, "While the Arabs do

----

[41] Early grammarians considered the imperative essentially a part of the imperfect (עתיד); so *Diq. ha-Ṭe'am.*, 35: ותאמר על הזמן העתיד אם תהיה מצוָּה; דִּבֶּר דברי דברו וכאשר תהיה מחנָה ומדמה תאמר ידבר ידברו תדברנה; Ibn Janāḥ (*Luma'*, 150, 15 ff.), in his explanation why the vowel of the middle radical in the imperative is in most instances the same as that of the imperfect, states: פאנך אנמא תאמר ממא לם יקע; also Ibn Ezra (*Moznayim*, Hamburg, 1770, 33h) and Qimhi (*Miklol*, ed. Lyck, 33b) include the imperative in their discussion of the imperfect. However, already Sībawaihi, I, 1, 4 f., states:

واما بناء ما لم يقع فانه قولك آمرا اذهب واقتل واضرب ومخبرا يقتل ويذهب, "As for the construction of what did not happen (the future), it is as you say commanding: 'Go!' etc., and informing: 'he will kill', etc." It is substantially the same as Ben Asher's statement, cited above.

[42] Dunash adds to this number four more simple forms (המילות הפשוטות), construed by analogy with עשִׂיתָנִי (Ezek. 29.3), which is considered by Saadia "an absurd expression" (see later); they are אשמעני, השמעתיני, שמעתיני, אשמיעני, thus making the number of simple forms 52. See *Teshubot*, No. 113, followed by No. 111, as corrected by the editor.

say, 'I found myself,' 'I taught myself,' thus joining the 1st per.
with the objective suffix of the 1st per., the Hebrews have not
sanctioned such usage, and its only instance in the Bible is
וַאֲנִי עֲשִׂיתִנִי (Ezek. 29.3), for they consider it an absurd expression." This view is vigorously disputed by Dunash who cites
the entire passage.[43] Several formations with objective suffixes
are illustrated by Saadia with examples from the Bible.

Here the mansucript breaks off, then resumes in an another
fragment of this part with a discussion of similar verbal forms
differing from each other only by one vowel, as שָׁמְעוּ and שִׁמְעוּ,
קוּמוּ and קוּמָו, or in the shift of tone, as בָּאָה (Gen. 15.17) and
בָּאָה (ibid. 29.6), קוּמִי (ibid. 21.18) and קוּמִי (Zeph. 3.8), etc.

Changes in verbal forms may be of three kinds: (1) In tenses
but not in numbers, as שמעת and תשמע; (2) In numbers but
not in tenses, as תשמע and תשמעו, and (3) In tenses and in
numbers, as שמעת and שָׁמְעוּ, where the change is from the past
to the present[44] and from the sing. to the pl. But in every
instance the change (אלתגׄיר) must take place in the same
person, whether 1st, 2nd, or 3rd, no matter what number. However, when the change is in the tenses and from one person to
another (as from 2nd to 3rd, or vice versa), then they are considered opposites (אצׄדאד), as שָׁמַע and שְׁמַע, where the change
is from the past to the present and from the 3rd to the 2nd
per., though both sing.

Then there are two forms, identical in every respect yet
different in meaning, as, e. g., תשמעני — תשמע may be the

<hr>

[43] *Ibid.*, No. 102. Similarly Ibn Janāḥ (*Lumaʿ*, 196, 5 ff.), Ibn Ezra (*Ṣaḥot*,
45b), and Qimḥi (*Miklol*, 27b) allow formations like שמרתיני, הכיתיני. For
the interpretation of עֲשִׂיתִנִי (Ezek. 29.3) see Targum, Rashi, Qimḥi, Menaḥem
b. Simon (ed. Barol, Berlin 1907, 57), Moses b. Sheshet, and Eliezer of
Beaugency, *ad loc.*

[44] Here and later Saadia associates the imperative with the present tense,
though previously, in arranging the conjugation, he included it with the
imperfect; see n. 41, above.

future sing. of either 2nd per. mas. or 3rd per. fem.; הוֹשִׁיבוּ may
be either 3rd per. pl. of the past or 2nd per. mas. pl. of the imperative, the same is the case with בּוֹשׁוּ (Isa. 45.16, Ezek. 36.32).
On the other hand, there are words different in form yet identical
in meaning, as, e. g., אוֹרוֹ (Isa. 13.10), אוֹרֵהוּ (Job 25.3); עִינָיו,
עִינֵיהוּ (ibid. 24.23); פָּרִים (2 Kings 19.29), פִּרְיְהֶם (Amos 9.14),
etc. The fragment ends here.

The conclusion of this part I was fortunate enough to identify
in a badly torn and rubbed off four-leaf fragment of the Taylor-
Schechter Collection of the Genizah at Cambridge University
Library. Beside a small portion of the end of this part, it
contains also a badly damaged text of the fourth part, which
appears to be a different version from the corresponding text
of the Leningrad fragments.

This conclusion contains the close of Saadia's discussion of
the number of the possible verbal forms. He states that in
accordance with his computation and including the forms of
אשתמע type[45] (*hitpaʻel*) there are approximately about 20,000
possible forms, but to be more exact there are 19,169 forms,
and he adds that he could not find one more form to make their
number 19,170, but it is impossible to enumerate them all.
Dunash who refers to this part as שער הצירוף quotes this
statement with amazement and mentions the *piʻel* forms, omitted
by Saadia, which would add a great many more verbal forms
to the number given by him.[46]

Saadia concludes this part with a suggestion how to find out
the form of a noun of verbs rarely used in the Scripture, whose
nominal forms are not found there. In such cases one should
find a similar verb and its nominal form more frequently in use
in the Bible, and by analogy construct the nominal form of the

---

[45] The study of אשתמע is not found in the identified fragments.
[46] *Teshubot*, Nos. 122, 123, also 102; cf. *Anfänge*, 54.

rarely used verb. So, e. g., the verb פִּצְחִי (Isa. 54.1), פִּצְחוּ (ibid. 44.23) has no nominal construction in the Bible, it should, therefore, be compared with the analogous verb שִׁמְעִי, שִׁמְעוּ, whose nominal form is שֵׁמַע (Gen. 29.13), hence the noun of the former should likewise be פֶּצַח. Similarly, מַשְׁעֵנָה (Isa. 3.1) may be compared with מַשְׁחֵתוֹ (Ezek. 9.1) whose noun is שַׁחַת, so the noun of the former should by analogy be שַׁעַן, and so is the case with other rarely used verbs. Finally, Saadia emphasizes that the general distinguishing characteristic of the noun from the verb is that the former takes the prefixes מ ל כ ב and the latter does not, for one cannot say כעברתי, בשמעתי. Scholars will know the distinction from preceding studies and definitions, but the common people will recognize it from this characteristic.[47]

IV. DAGESH AND RAFE

In the fourth part Saadia treats of the various aspects of *Dagesh* and *Rafe* (אלתשדיד ואלארכא). All the consonants of the alphabet, except א ה ח ע, may take a *dagesh*, but the six consonants ב ג ד כ פ ת have special characteristics in this respect. Thus the *resh* is included among the consonants that may take a *dagesh*, though with some qualifications.[48] Saadia maintains

<hr>

[47] The text of this part, with an English translation, was published in *JQR*, N. S., XXXIII, 171 ff. (*Saadia Studies*, Philadelphia, 1943, 63 ff.). However, since its publication two old torn parchment leaves belonging to it were identified in the Genizah, one at Cambridge University Library and the other at the Bodleian Library in Oxford, which contain a more complete and correct text than that of the Leningrad fragment, on which the edition is based. Besides, another short fragment, mentioned above, containing the end of this part (it will be described at the end of Part IV), was likewise identified by me at Cambridge, and, in addition, a two-leaf fragment misplaced in the Leningrad Ms. was also identified by me as belonging to it. So I am now considering the advisability of preparing a new edition of this part.

[48] Saadia gives the rules of *dagesh* in a *resh* in his Com. on *Sefer Yeṣirah* (79, 6 ff.; Translation, 102), as follows: If one of ת צ ס ס ט ז ד precedes the

that there are several instances of *dagesh* and *rafe* in words, especially in primitive nouns, where one cannot give a satisfactory explanation for them, as, e. g., עַמִּים and בָּנִים, or חִנָּם and חֵפֶץ, etc. In these and in many similar instances there is no particular reason why one word has a *dagesh* and the other is *rafe*. They are naturally inherent in some words and accepted to be so by usage, just as it is accepted that יוֹם should mean *day* and יָם — *sea*; if their meanings were reversed, it would not make any difference. Just as there is no special reason for the consonantal make-up of primitive nouns, so there is no particular reason for their vocalization, for in both cases they have been so accepted by usage. And similar is the case with the natural *dagesh* and *rafe* in primitive nouns, and one should not look for any special cause for them.

However, when the word is inflected or has prefixes or suffixes added to it, then there are reasons for its having a *dagesh* or being *rafe*. So when a verb is changed from intransitive to transitive it takes a *dagesh*, as, e. g., חָזַק changed to חִזַּק, לָמַד changed to לִמַּד; or when it is changed to denote a modification in meaning, as שָׁלַח *he sent* and שִׁלַּח *he sent away, set free*; or

---

resh and either this consonant or the *resh* has a *shewa*, then the *resh* takes a *dagesh*, as דַּרְכְּמוֹנִים (Ezra 2.69), דְּרוֹר (Ex. 30.23), וַאָזְרֵם בְּמִזְרֶה (Jer. 15.7), etc., but if both of them have vowels, the *resh* is *rafe*, as דרך יום (1 Kings 19.4), צְרִי (Gen. 43.11). If *lamed* or *nun* follow the *resh*, with no vowel between them (i. e. the *resh* has a *shewa*), then the *resh* takes a *dagesh*, as וְדִלְחוּ (*ibid.* 17.14), בְּרִנְנָה (Ps. 100.2); he then adds that these rules of *dagesh* and *rafe* of the *resh* are according to the Tiberians. Elsewhere Saadia states that the Tiberians observe the twofold pronunciation of the *resh* in the Bible, but the ‘Irāqians (Babylonians) observe it in their speech, but not in the Bible (Com. on *Sefer Yeṣirah*, 45, 4 f.).

These rules are also given by Ben Asher, with the modification that if the *resh* has a *shewa* after the six consonants, it it *rafe* (*Diq. ha-Ṭe‘am.*, 7 f.). See *Teshubot Talmide Menaḥem*, 71; *Luma‘*, 29, 9 ff.; 241, 6 ff.; *Ṣaḥot*, 31a; *Moonayim*, 22b, J. Qimḥi, *Zikkaron*, 10, 30 ff.; Moses of England, *Sefer ha-Shoham*, ed. Klar, 19, 23 f.; *Miklol*, 57a, 81b f.; *Eine hebr. Grammatik aus d. XIII Jh.*, ed. Poznański, 10, and n. 29; Gumpertz, *Tarbiz*, XVI, 223 ff.

when the verb denoting a single action is changed to denote a repeated action, as רָצַח and רִצַּח, or an intensive action, as שָׁבַר and שִׁבַּר. In all these and similar instances there is a distinct modification in meaning.

Then follows a detailed study of *dagesh* and *rafe* after each of the seven prefixes שׁ מ ל כ ו ה ב. So there is a *dagesh* after ל כ ב in definite nouns and *rafe* in indefinite ones, as בַּבַּיִת — בְּבַיִת, כַּיּוֹם — כְּיוֹם, לַלֶּחֶם — לְלֶחֶם. After a *he* there is *dagesh* in an affirmative (אלאתבאת — definite), as הַבָּנִים, and a *rafe* in a negative (אלנפי), as הֲבָנִים אֵין לְיִשְׂרָאֵל (Jer. 49.1), or in an interrogative (אלאסתפהאם), as הֲגוֹי גַּם צַדִּיק (Gen. 20.4); but if the first consonant of the noun has a *shewa*, it takes a *dagesh* also in an interrogative, as הַבְּרָב־כֹּחַ (Job 23.6), except הַבְּסוֹד (ibid. 15.8), which is *rafe* with a *shewa*.[49] After a *waw* there is a *dagesh* in a *yod*, *nun*, and *taw* in verbal forms of the past and a *rafe* in those of the future, as וַיַּעַשׂ, וְיַעַשׂ (Dan. 11.16); וַנִּשְׁמַע (Josh. 2.11), וְנִשְׁמָע (Ex. 24.7); וַתְּחִי (Gen. 45.27), וּתְחִי (Isa. 55.3). After a *mem* all nouns, except those beginning with ע ח ה א and also ר, take a *dagesh*, as מִמָּחֳרָת (Gen. 19.34), מִנֶּגַהּ (2 Sam. 22.13), etc., except מִגְּבוּרָתָם[50] (Ezek. 32.30). After a *shin* all the 18 consonants, including the *resh*, take a *dagesh*, as שֶׁכָּכָה השבעתנו (Cant. 5.9), שֶׁשְּׁזָפַתְנִי (ibid. 1.6), and in a *resh* שֶׁרֹּאשִׁי (ibid. 5.2).

At the end of the word *dagesh* and *rafe* occur in the pronominal suffixes *nun*, *kaf*, and *taw*. When the suffix is a *nun* and is followed by a *yod* (objective suffix of 1st per.), in most instances it is *rafe*, as וְחָנֵּנִי (Ps. 25.16), etc., but with some exceptions, as הִנֵּנִי בני (Gen. 22.7), דָּנַנִּי[51] (ibid. 30.6), מִמֶּנִּי,[52] etc., which have

[49] See *Teshubot*, Nos. 108d and 120; *Luma'*, 357, 18 ff., and *Miklol*, 48a ff., for several more instances.

[50] Cf. *Jāmi' al-Alfāẓ*, II, 180, 14 f.; *Luma'*, 276, 7 ff.; J. Qimḥi, *Zikkaron*, 12, 19 f., and *Miklol*, 41a.

[51] See *Luma'*, 73, 22; *Zikkaron*, 9, 15 f., 25 f., and *Miklol*, 5a.

[52] See *Abraham ibn Ezra als Grammatiker*, 150, for a quotation from *Yesod Diqduq* about the *dagesh* in the *nun* in מִמֶּנִּי, and *Ṣaḥot*, 29b.

a *dagesh*; when the *nun* is followed by a *he*, it is *rafe* in the imperfect 2nd and 3rd per. pl. fem., as יִדיו תְּבִיאֶינָה (Lev. 7.30), but if it is an objective suffix of the 3rd per. fem sing., the *nun* takes a *dagesh*, as מֶרבכת תביאֶנָּה[53] (ibid. 6.14); when the *nun* is followed by a *waw*, it is *rafe* in objective suffixes of 1st per. pl., as חָנֵּנוּ י"י חָנֵּנוּ (Ps. 123.3), except three instances of הִנֶּנּוּ (Gen. 44.16, 50.18; Num. 14.40) which have a *dagesh* in 1st per. pl., but the *nun* takes a *dagesh* in objective suffixes of the 3rd per. sing., as תִּשְׁפְּכֶנּוּ (Deut. 12.16), תאכלנו[54] (ibid. 28.39); similarly all instances of [אֵינֶנּוּ][55] have a *dagesh*, no matter whether 1st per. pl. or 3rd per. sing. masc.; but ממנו has a *dagesh* when it is 3rd per. sing., as מִמֶּנּוּ פנה מִמֶּנּוּ יתד (Zech. 10.4), and is *rafe* when it is 1st per. pl., as כי עצמת מִמֶּנּוּ (Gen. 26.16). In this vocalization of ממנו Saadia follows the Oriental, or Babylonian, school (מדנחאי), who vocalize it with a *ṣere* followed by *rafe*, for the Occidental, or Palestinian, school (מערבאי) vocalize it with a *segol* and *dagesh*.[56]

The *kaf* when added to nouns, singular or plural, and preceded by a *segol* is usually *rafe*, but there are exceptions, as אכל דַיֶּךָ (Prov. 25.16). When the *kaf* is added to verbs in the imperfect 1st and 3rd per. sing., it takes a *dagesh* in some instances, when preceded by a *segol*, as וַאֲבָרְכֶךָ (Gen. 26.3), ולא אעזבֶךָּ (Josh. 1.5), ויברכֶךָ, ויעזרֶךָ (Gen. 49.25), etc., except אצֻוֶּךָ (1 Kings 11.38), אשביעֶךָ (Ps. 81.17), etc., which are *rafe*; also מצַוֶּךָ (Deut. 12.14, 28) has a *dagesh*.[57] The passage containing the discussion of *dagesh* and *rafe* in suffixed *taw* is badly destroyed,

---

[53] *Diq. ha-Ṭe'am.*, § 55; *Jāmi' al-Alfāẓ*, II, 242, 46 ff.; Ḥayyūj, *Nutaf*, ed. Kokowzoff, 44 (Translation, 36 ff.); *Luma'*, 242, 9 f., and *Miklol*, 34b, 79a.

[54] See *Jāmi' al-Alfāẓ*, II, 241, 33 ff.; *Ṣaḥot*, 29b, and *Zikkaron*, 9, 24 f.

[55] This word is destroyed in the Ms., restored by conjecture.

[56] Cf. Geiger in *Kerem Ḥemed*, IX, 69, and Pinsker, מבוא אל הנקוד האשורי, 2; for Ibn Ezra's objection to the Babylonian vocalization, see his Commentary on Gen. 3.22.

[57] Cf. *Jāmi' al-Alfāẓ*, II, 79, 45 ff.

and the scant information that could be gathered from it is that it has reference to the 2nd per. perfect.

In his study of the spirants ת פ כ ד ג ב Saadia advances three premises: (1) When one of these consonants has no *dagesh*, it is lightened in pronunciation and its place of origin in the mouth is changed. (2) They take a *dagesh* more frequently than other consonants for reasons that preclude their being *rafe*. (3) There are a number of words beginning with one of the spirants that have a *dagesh* for no linguistic reason, and they have to be carefully studied.

When two words are joined by a conjunctive accent, the first ending with a vowel and the second beginning with one of ת פ כ ד ג ב, it is aspirated, as עֵינֵי כֹל (Ps. 145.15), וִיבָטְחוּ בְךָ (ibid. 9.11). In this connection Saadia maintains that words ending in ה י ו א do not necessarily aspirate these consonants, as alleged by many scholars,[58] for if it were so they would have aspirated them even when the former are not quiescent, as, e. g., יְ שְׂפָתַי (Job 22.22), קח נא מִפִּיו תוֹרָה (Gen. 6.16), בְּצֹהֲרָה תָשִׂים תִּפְתָּח (Ps. 51.17). But since ת פ כ ד ג ב have a *dagesh* in all such instances, the rule should be formulated that these consonants are aspirated only when the preceding word ends in a vowel (an open syllable) and have a *dagesh* when preceded by a word ending in a consonant (a closed syllable).

The reasons that preclude the spirantization of these consonants are three: (1) The rules that necessitate having a *dagesh* in other consonants govern these too, as לָמָה בָּאתִי (2 Sam. 14.32), אֶקְרָה כֹּה[59] (Num. 23.15). (2) When the two consonants כ ב

---

[58] Evidently referring to Ben Asher, see *Diq. ha-Ṭe'am.*, § 29, where the *dagesh* and *rafe* in ת פ כ ד ג ב is discussed at length.

[59] Both instances are what is termed אתי מרחיק, when a word ending in a toneless syllable with הָ— or הֶ— is connected with a word having the tone on the first syllable or with a monosyllabic word; see *ibid.*; *Kitāb al-Lin*, 12 f.;

or פ ב occur in the beginning of the word and the first has a *shewa*, it takes a *dagesh*, as וַיְהִי בְּבוֹאָם (1 Sam. 16.6), הֲלֹא כְּכַרְכְּמִישׁ (Isa. 10.9), לֹא יִרְדֶּנּוּ בְּפָרֶךְ (Lev. 25.53). (3) When any three of ת פ כ ד ג ב occur in the beginning of the word and the first has a *shewa*, it takes a *dagesh*, as אדרגזריא גְּדָבְרִיא דְתָבְרִיא (Dan. 3.2).

Then there are words beginning with one of these consonants that take a *dagesh* for no particular linguistic reason; among them are four in the Song of the Red Sea: מִי כָּמֹכָה (Ex. 15.11), the two instances of כִּי גָאֹה גָּאָה (ibid. 1, 21), and יִדְמוּ כָּאָבֶן (ibid. 16); also וְנִלְאֵיתִי כַּלְכֵל (Jer. 20.9), ושמתי כַּדְכֹד (Isa. 54.12), and every instance of [60]וַיְהִי כִּשְׁמֹעַ (Gen. 29.13+),— all these and similar cases have a *dagesh* and are exceptions to the previously mentioned rules.

This part ends here according to the fragments of the Leningrad Ms., but the fragment identified by me in summer, 1948, at the Taylor-Schechter Collection of the Genizah in Cambridge contains a more comprehensive version of it. Unfortunately, the lower portion of the fragment is torn off and parts of the remaining text are obliterated and often quite illegible. It is interesting to note that the material here is differently arranged

Miklol, 80a ff., and *Grammaire hébr.*, ed. Neubauer, 10 ff., for an adequate discussion of these consonants.

[60] This is the reading of Ben Naftali, Ben Asher reads the *kaf rafe*, see *Diq. hu-Ṭe'am.*, p. 30, 11. This difference of opinion is called attention to in *Grammaire hébr.*, 11; see also *Minḥat Shai* on Judg. 7. 15. Bacher (*Anfänge*, 46) cites Saadia's reading and observes that it is contrary to the masoretic punctuation, but fails to identify it with Ben Naftali's reading, whom the Gaon appears to follow. It is interesting to note that Norzi (*Minḥat Shai* on Judg. 7. 15) states: מדקדוק 'ברוב הספרים הכ"ף דגושה ומצאתי כתוב בספר א מדקדוק ישן כ"י זה הכלל כל ויהי של תלשא קטנה וראש תיבה שלאחריו כ"ף היא נדגשת כגון ויהי כראות המלך (אסתר ה, ב)... ויהי כשמוע לבן (בראשית כ"ט, י"נ) וכן הרבה ומפני הוגן הקריאה תקנו לבטל חוק יהו"א. Yet all our texts, as Miqra'ot Gedolot, Baer, Ginsburg, and Kittel, have the *kaf rafe*.

and more amplified than that of the Leningrad fragments; even
many of the examples from the Bible are different.

The four-leaf fragment contains the end of Part III, as
previously mentioned, and what appears to be the greater part
of Part IV, which begins in the middle of fol. 1a with אלמקאלה
אלראבעה מן אלי״ב מקאלה אלתי הי גמלה כתאב פציח אלעבראני
ואעראבה קול פי אלמשדّד ואלמרכّי אלמסמّי באלעבראניّה דגש
ורפי, "The fourth treatise of the twelve treatises which embrace
the Book of Elegance of Hebrew, and it comprises a Discourse
on the Strengthened and Weakened [Letters], called in Hebrew
Dagesh and Rafe." The text is very fragmentary but much
more comprehensive than that of the Leningrad fragments.
This part ends with תّם אלכתאב בעון אללה אלמחסן at the lower
half of fol. 3b. Then another treatise of Saadia begins, bearing
the title: אלקול פי אלסראג אלדׁי יסרג מן יום אלגّמעה ללסבת,
"Discourse on the Light that is Kindled on Friday for the
Sabbath."[61] It extends from the rest of fol. 3b to the end of the
fragment on fol. 4b. So far as I am aware, this is the only
fragment of the text of this treatise that has been identified.
On fol. 4b Saadia makes reference to another work of his: כמא
שרחת פי כתאב דפע אלקיאס פי אלפראיׁץ אלסמעיّה באתّסאע,
"As I have explained at length in the 'Book of Rejection of
Analogy in (the interpretation of) the Revealed Precepts'
(transmitted by tradition)."[62] But I hope to publish a study
of this fragment on another occasion.

[61] See Malter, *Saadia Gaon*, 399 f.; *Genizah Studies*, II, ed. Ginzberg, 487 ff.,
and Abramson in ספר הזכרון לבית המדרש לרבנים בוינה, 1940, 155 ff., 169.
This definitely establishes that it was a separate treatise and not a part of
Saadia's *Kitāb al-Tamyīz*, as Poznański thinks, cited by Malter, *op. cit.*, 400.

[62] Cf. *ibid.*, 400 f,; perhaps it is to be identified with פי אלקיאס אבטאל
אלשראיׁע אלסמעיّה, as cited by Poznański, *Karaite Liter. Oppon.*, 97, who
suggests that אלקיאס should be read אלקّיאם, followed by Malter. The
reading in the present Ms. is not entirely clear, but אלקיאס is mentioned a

However, apart from the afore-mentioned fragments of Part IV there are several brief rules of *dagesh* and *rafe*, cited by Saadia from this part in his Commentary on *Sefer Yeṣirah*. He emphasizes there that the spirantization of ת פ כ ד ג ב occurs not only in biblical usage, but also in everyday speech and in conversation of women. So when one of them wished the teacher to free her son, she asked him in Aramaic: יא ספרא אפני בְּרִי, with an aspirated ב, and when another woman called her son גַּד גַּד, he did not respond, so she called again יא גָד, with an aspirated ג because of יא, and he understood her.[63] Almost all the rules, cited by him, are discussed in the preceding study. Among them Saadia mentions that these consonants are aspirated after a word ending in a vowel (an open syllable), except a *pataḥ*, in which case they take a *dagesh*, as מַה־בָּצַע (Gen. 37.26). The Cambridge fragment has a similar example: מַה־כֹּחִי (Job 6.11), alongside with מַה־טֹּבוּ (Num. 24.5) and ונפתחה־בָּר (Amos 8.5), but the text is partially destroyed, and it is not quite clear what rule these examples were intended to illustrate; perhaps דאתי מרחיק, as maintained by Ben Asher.[64] The three exceptions of מפיק followed by *rafe*: קַו־תָהוּ (Isa. 34.11), שָׁלְוּ בָה (Ezek. 23.42), אדנָי בָם (Ps. 68.18), are likewise mentioned in this fragment.

Also Dunash cites several rules of *dagesh* and *rafe* from this

few times in it in connection with the title, as seen from the following quotation: ... אלכפאר ודוי אלגנאחאת אלכבאיר והם בצלם אל״ים איצא פלמא חכם אלנגֹ בדפע מא תעבה (=תבעה) ג פנון אלקיאס תרי אן אלשראיע אלנבריֿה ליסת עלי קיאס הי מוצועהֿ כמא שרחת פי כתאב דפע אלקיאס פי אלפראיץ אלסמעיֿה באחֿסאע אלא אני ארי הדה אלה קיאסאת מנכסרהֿ גיר מתבתהֿ אלךֹ. As one can readily see, Saadia discusses here the rejection of Analogy (אלקיאס).

[63] *Commentaire sur le Séfer Yeṣira*, 45, 9 ff.

[64] *Diq. ha-Ṭeʿam.*, p. 29, 7 f.; וכל מה דסמיך לבנדרכפ״ת במקף נידון כאתי מרחיק לעולם, כמו מַה־בָּצַע (בראשית ל״ז, כ״ו); cf. *Miklol*, 80a, where this and similar examples are cited as illustrations of דחיק; similarly *Grammaire hébr.*, 12, 15 ff.

part which he mentions by name,[65] some of which are missing in
the fragments so far identified. Among the latter is the irregular
rafe in the *pi'el* forms וּבַקְשׁוּ (Jer. 5.1) and בְּקְשׁוּ[66] (Esth. 6.2,
Ezra 2.62, Nehem. 7.64); the *rafe* of the *yod* with a *shewa* in
definite nouns, as הַיְלדים (Gen. 33.1), הַיְתרים (Judg. 16.9),
הַיְשׁוּעָה (1 Sam. 14.45), except הַיְּוָנִים (Joel 4.6) which has a
dagesh, and a number of similar instances of *rafe* in definite
nouns mentioned by Dunash are missing in the fragments.[67]
But the examples of *rafe* of the *mem* in the definite participial forms like הַמְהלך, הַמְקָרה (Ps. 104.3), and likewise
the difference between the non-pausal הַמְלֵאָה הזרע (Deut.
22.9) which is *rafe* and the pausal בבטן הַמְלֵאָה (Eccl. 11.5)
which has a *dagesh*, as well as other instances of *rafe* in
definite nouns cited by Dunash,[68] are all found in the Cambridge
fragment. Dunash brings also another case of *rafe* after a *mem*:
מִבְצִיר (Judg. 8.2) in addition to מִגְבוּרָתָם (Ezek. 32.30), and
many more instances of *rafe* in nouns with the interrogative *he*
followed by a *shewa* than the single instance of הַבְסוֹד (Job 15.8),
given by Saadia, as previously mentioned.[69] In this connection
Bacher remarks that one can see that Saadia was not as thor-
oughly familiar with the entire range of masoretic material as
the masorete Ben Asher and Dunash who was also well versed
in this subject.[70] However, one gains the impression that the
Gaon, in his presentation of Hebrew grammar, never intended
utilizing all the masoretic material, with the complete lists of
rules and exceptions, with which he was no doubt quite familiar.

---

[65] *Teshubot*, No. 120.

[66] *Ibid.*, No. 108b, also No. 108c, where לָמֶּה with a *dagesh* and לָמָה *rafe*
are cited, see *Diq. ha-Ṭe'am.*, § 56; *Jāmi' al-Alfāẓ*, II, 168, 16 ff.; *Miklol*, 193a;
Grammaire hébr., 21, 10 ff.

[67] *Teshubot*, No. 108e–f; see *Ṣaḥot*, 17b, and *Miklol*, 41a.

[68] *Teshubot*, No. 108g–k; see *Miklol, l. c.*

[69] See nn. 49 and 50, above.

[70] *Anfänge*, 47.

V. The Vowels[71]

Saadia begins his study of vowels (אלקול פי אלנגם) with a brief general introduction consisting of four premises, of which only three are given in the Leningrad manuscript. They are as follows: (1) An utterance cannot begin with a vowel but with a consonantal sound, for no sound can possibly begin with a vowel without a consonant preceding it. (2) When a speaker begins an utterance with a consonant it must necessarily be followed by a vowel, for no consonant can be pronounced by itself. (3) A vowel following a consonant may be followed by a second or more consonants, for it is possible that the utterance either stops with the given vowel or the latter is followed by one or more consonants.

Here is a lacuna in the Ms., which resumes with a study of the origin of the seven vowels in the mouth, in consecutive order of the positions of their enunciation as they ascend from the throat. So the first vowel sound ascending from the throat is the *holem*, and its force moves directly straightforward, without deviating upward or downward. The vowel sound beyond that position is the *qames*, its movement being toward the upper palate. The position of the vowel sound after this is that of the *patah*, its force going forth over the surface of the tongue and descending below. The *segol* is in the very same position, its force comprising both lower sides of the mouth. When the vowel sound passes beyond this position, approaching the tip of the

---

[71] The following survey of Part V is rather brief in view of the fact that an edition of its Arabic text so far extant, with an English translation and notes, has recently appeared in *JQR*, N. S., XLII, 233 ff., bearing the title "A Study of Hebrew Vowels from Saadia Gaon's Grammatical Work 'Kutuh al-Lughah'." It was, therefore, deemed unnecessary to reiterate here the critical study which is now readily available to the interested scholar.

tongue to the teeth without covering them, the *ṣere* appears, but when it covers the teeth the *ḥireq* becomes audible. These two vowels are enunciated inside the mouth near the teeth. But if the vowel sound passes beyond these positions and comes out between the lips and the teeth, the *shureq* appears. Thus, the consecutive order of the positions of the vowels in the mouth is *ḥolem, qameṣ, pataḥ, segol, ṣere, ḥireq*, and *shureq*.

Saadia presents now a study of the possibility of combination of the vowels with each other. In this he follows the method he pursued with regard to the 22 letters of the alphabet in the first part of this Grammar.[72] Besides, if there be any doubt about the vocalization of some consonant, it could be deduced from the adjoining vowel, whether it could combine with the one in doubt or not, and thus help to clear the matter up. The study of these combinations of vowels is systematically arranged and profusely illustrated with quotations from the Bible, enumerating in consecutive order such combinations of every vowel with each other as are possible, both in stems and in inflected forms. So a *ḥolem* adjoins a *ḥolem* in a stem, as אוֹנוֹ (Nehem. 6.2) which is a name of a town, and in an inflected form, as אוֹרוֹ; it adjoins a *qameṣ* in a stem, as טוֹבָה, and in an inflected form, as הוֹדָה; it adjoins a *pataḥ* in a stem, as רֹמַח (Num. 25.7), and in an inflected form, as וַאֹכַל (Gen. 27.33), and so forth, with every vowel as it adjoins, or not, another vowel in stems and in inflected forms.

This is followed by a study of vowel changes from a higher to a lower position in descending order. The study is limited to the six vowels whose positions are inside the mouth, omitting the *shureq* which is enunciated outside the mouth, between the teeth and the lips. There are four causes for raising or lowering

---

[72] See the study of this part, *Proceedings*, XXI, 79 ff. [5 ff.].

the vowels in their positions. They are: the plural, as, e. g.,
בֶּן — בָּנִים, אָח — אַחִים; the construct state (including nouns
with possessive suffixes), as, e. g., בֵּית י"י — בַּיִת (Ex. 23.19);
tense formations, as, e. g., תֹּאמְרוּ, אָמַרְתִּי — אוֹמֵר; and pausal
forms, as, e. g., עֶשֶׂר יָדוֹת (2 Sam. 19.44), עָרִים עֶשֶׂר [73] (Josh. 21.5).
Such vocalic changes to a higher or lower position are brought
about in the above-mentioned order, in some instances by all
the four causes, in other instances by three, in still others — by
two, or by one cause, in accordance with the usage of the Hebrew
language. So the change from *holem* to *qames*, as עֹמֶר (Lev.
23.15) is in the plural בֵּין הָעֳמָרִים (Ruth 2.15); גֹּבַהּ is with a
possessive suffix כְּגֹבַהּ אֲרָזִים גָּבְהוֹ (Amos 2.9). The change from
qames to *patah*, as, e. g., יַד הָעֵדִים — יָד (Deut. 17.7) in the
construct state, etc. The change from *patah* to *segol*, as, e. g.,
אֶמְצָאֲךָ (Cant. 8.1) becomes in the 3rd per. pausal form לֹא
יִמְצָאֶכָה (1 Kings 13.10), and so are the changes with other
vowels.

Similar changes take place likewise in ascending order, and
for the same causes, as from *hireq* to *sere*: דְּרָכִים is דַּרְכֵי in the
construct state; from *sere* to *segol*: בֶּן — בֶּן־יִצְהָר (1 Chron. 6.23),
etc. Such changes in ascending or descending order may involve
one or more of them, as וַיֵּלֶךְ (Ex. 4.18) changes in pause to
וַיֵּלַךְ (Gen. 24.61+), involving one change, but in אֶרֶץ — אָרֶץ
there are two consecutive changes, first from *segol* to *patah*,
which, in turn, changes to *qames*, thus the *segol* is changed to a
qames which replaces the *patah*.

The unique Leningrad fragment breaks off with the beginning
of the discussion of shortening and lengthening of vowels. So
the *holem* may be shortened, lengthened, or changed into *qames*.

____

[73] Cf. *Diq. ha-Te'am.*, p. 35, 2 ff., where only three causes for vowel changes
are given, omitting the pausal forms mentioned here.

The change into *qameṣ* occurs when the word following it begins with a tone-bearing syllable, as יַעֲמָד־נָא (1 Sam. 16.22), יִזְכָּר־נָא (2 Sam. 14.11). It is a great pity that the fragment should end at this very interesting point.

VI. The Shewa

In this part Saadia treats of the various aspects of the *shewa* (אלגזם), quiescent and vocal (סאכנה ומתחרّכה). The fragments begin with the rule that when there are two *shewas* in the middle of the word, the first is quiescent and the second is vocal, as מַחְשְׁבֹת (Gen. 6.5), תִּתְקְפֵהוּ (Job 14.20). Then follows a study of the instances when a vocal *shewa* is pronounced like a *patah*.[74] The following rules about it are preserved in the fragment: (1) When the consonant with the *shewa* has a *dagesh*, as וַאֲסַלְּדָה (Job 6.10), וְהִתְעַנְּגוּ[75] (Ps. 37.11), etc. (2) When the *shewa* is between a *ma'arikha* and a *shofar* (*munah*), or similar conjunctive accents, as נְדָרוּ (Ps. 76.12), תְּלָעֲג[76] (Prov. 30.17), etc. (3) When the second vowel after the *shewa* is tone-bearing and has a *dagesh*, as נֵלְכָה־נָא (Ex. 3.18), נוֹתְרָה־בָּה[77] (Ezek. 14.22); for this reason the *shewa* of the *zayin* in יְשֵׁיזְבִנָּךְ[77a] (Dan. 6.17) is

[74] See *JQR*, N. S., XLII, 287, n. 18, for references to early grammarians who maintained that a vocal *shewa* before non-laryngeals (but not before a *yod*) is pronounced like a *patah*; see also Ḥayyūj, *Niqqud*, ed. Nutt, 130, 13 ff.; Levy, *Zur masoret. Grammatik*, texts, 4, 12 f., and *'Et Sofer*, 4a. But cf. M. Qimḥi, *Mahalak*, 13b, that in all such instances: קריאת השוא נוטה לקמץ.

[75] *Diq. ha-Ṭe'am.*, p. 13, 5 f.; *Niqqud*, 130, 17 f.; *Grammaire hébr.*, 19, 3; Levy, *op. cit.*, 18, 4 ff.; Almoli, *Halikot Sheva*, 20.

[76] *Niqqud*, 130, 21 f.; *Miklol*, 15a, 137a; *Grammaire hébr.*, 18, 16 ff. Cf. *Diq. ha-Ṭe'am.*, § 27; *Jāmi' al-Alfāẓ*, II, 684, 96 ff., and Levy, *op. cit.*, 14, 4 ff., for the opinion that this rule applies only to the three books Psalms, Proverbs, and Job; cf. also *Minhat Shai* on Ps. 86.2.

[77] Cf. *Diq. ha-Ṭe'am.*, § 50; *Niqqud*, 130, 23 f.; Levy, *op. cit.*, 15, 10 ff.

[77a] The edited text of Ḥayyūj, *Niqqud*, in both the Dukes (201, 7) and the Nutt (130, 25) editions, has erroneously לשיזבותנא (Dan. 3, 17), where

vocal, but in יְשֵׁיזְבִנְכוֹן (ibid. 3.15) it is quiescent, because in the
former case the *nun* has a *dagesh* but in the latter — the *nun* is
rafe. (4) When there are the same two consonants in the middle
of the word, which are preceded by a lengthened vowel, and the
first of these consonants has a *shewa*, as וִיסוֹבְבוּ (Ps. 59.7),
דְּלֲלוּ (Isa. 19.6), etc., but if the preceding vowel is short, the
shewa is not vocal, as וְשָׁדְדוּ את בני קדם[78] (Jer. 49.28). (5) when
the *shewa* is on a *mem* and the second vowel (אלנגמה אלתאניה,
i. e. the second vocalized consonant) after it is tone-bearing, as
הַמְכַסֶּה (Gen. 18.17), הַמְהַלֵּךְ (Ps. 104.3), etc., but [not][79] in
הַמְהַלְּכִים (Eccl. 4.15).

Here is a lacuna in the fragments, which resume with the end
of the discussion of the last of the five rules of the *shewa* before
the laryngeals ע ח ה א, which is pronounced like the vowel of
the latter, viz., when the second syllable after the *shewa* has a
dagesh and is tone-bearing, the *shewa* is pronounced like the vowel
of the laryngeal following it, as נפשו יָרְעָה לּוֹ[80] (Isa. 15.4). But
when two of the same, or different, laryngeals follow each other
in the middle of the word and the first has a *shewa*, it is pronounced like a *patah* and not like the vowel of the second laryngeal, as יְתְרוֹעֲעוּ (Ps. 65.14), שָׁחֲחוּ (Job 9.13), יִמְחָאוּ־כָף[81] (Ps.

the *zayin* has a *qames* and not a *shewa*, instead of the correct ישיזבנך given
here.

[78] *Diq. ha-Ṭe‘am.*, § 33; *Niqqud*, ed. Nutt, 130, 18 ff.; *Grammaire hébr.*,
18, 3 ff.; Levy, *op. cit.*, 15, 18 ff.; *Halikot Sheva*, 45 f.

[79] Restored word conjectural, for there is a lacuna in the Ms. Cf. *Diq.
ha-Ṭe‘am.*, § 34; *Niqqud*, 130, 26 ff.; *Miklol*, 41a; *Grammaire hébr.*, 17, 25 ff.;
Levy, *op. cit.*, 29.

[80] See *Diq. ha-Ṭe‘am.*, § 14; *Kitāb al-Līn*, 5, 6 ff., and *Niqqud*, 130, 32 ff.;
Ṣahot, 2a; *Zikkaron*, 18, 11 ff.; M. Qimḥi, *Mahalak*, 13a; *Miklol*, 138b;
Grammaire hébr., 19, 6 ff.; Levy, *op. cit.*, 18, 11 ff.; Almoli, *Halikot Sheva*, 25 f.
Saadia mentions this rule also in his Commentary on *Sefer Yeṣirah*, 76, 11 f.
(Translation, 98). Ibn Ezra (*Moznayim*, 27a) cites this rule in the name
of Ḥayyūj, then adds: ויאמרו כי כן ואנשי טבריא.

[81] *Niqqud*, 131, 5 ff.; *Grammaire hébr.*, 19, 19 ff.; Levy, *op. cit.*, 23.

98.8). Also when the *shewa* is on a *mem* before a laryngeal and
the tone is on the second vowel after the *shewa*, the latter is
pronounced like a *patah*, as הַמְחַכִּים (Job 3.21), הַמְהַלֵּךְ[82] (Ps.
104.3).

A vocal *shewa* before a *yod* is invariably pronounced like *hireq*,
no matter what vowel the *yod* has, as וְיוֹם (Gen. 8.22), the *waw*
is pronounced with a *hireq* although the *yod* has *holem*; or כִּיָרֵחַ
(Ps. 89.38), the *yod* has a *qames* but the *kaf* is pronounced with a
hireq, and so in similar instances.[83] With this Saadia concludes
his study of the quiescent and vocal *shewas*, when the latter is
pronounced like a *patah* or *hireq*, and when it is assimilated to
the seven vowels following it.

Now follows a study of the changes that take place in non-
pausal and pausal forms with regard to the *shewa*. But, unfortunately, here again is a lacuna in the fragments, which resume
with instances where a *holem* replaces the *shewa* in pause, as
זְכָרוּ (Isa. 46.8), זִכְרוּ (Nehem. 4.8), thus reverting to the original
vowel in זְכוֹר, as is also the case with עָמְדוּ עָמָדוּ (Nah. 2.9),

[82] Cf. *Niqqud*, 131, 7 f.: והאחד שיהיה השוא עם אות דגוש אז לא יהיה כנוע הפתח
כמו המהלך וזהו כמו שרש כי אין תולדתו כי אם פתח, the meaning seems
to be that if the *mem* with a *shewa* before a laryngeal has a *dagesh*, it is not
considered any longer a *vocal shewa* which is *pronounced like* a *patah*, but
is virtually a regular *patah*. But the *mem* in המהלך (Ps. 104.3) is *rafe*, though
it has a *dagesh* in the Dukes edition (p. 202, 11); in fact, Saadia used it above
as an example of a *mem* with *shewa* pronounced like *patah*, alongside with
המכסה (Gen. 18.17), also without a *dagesh*, see n. 79, above.

[83] *Diq. ha-Te'am.*, § 12; *Kitāb al-Līn*, 6, 3 ff., and *Niqqud*, 131, 9 ff.;
Sahot, 2a; *Zikkaron*, 18, 22 ff.; M. Qimhi, *Mahalak*, 13a f.; *Miklol*, 138b f.;
'Et Sofer, 4a; *Grammaire hébr.*, 19, 25 ff.; Levy, *op. cit.*, 21, n. 3. Ibn Ezra
(*Sahot*, *l. c.*) cites Hayyūj that the Tiberians read a vocal *shewa* before a
yod with a *hireq*, but neither the Jastrow edition of *Kitāb al-Līn* nor Ibn Ezra's
own translation of this work and of *Kitāb al-Tanqīt*, (ed. Dukes, 5, 7 ff.;
202, 13 f.) mention the Tiberians in this connection, see Bacher, *Abr. ibn
Ezra als Grammatiker*, 37, n. 6. Also Almoli (*Halikot Sheva*, ed. Yallon, 23 f.)
quotes this statement, most likely from *Sahot*; see editor's n. 61, *ad loc.*.
and references given there.

where the first is non-pausal and the second is pausal. Similarly
חֲדַל־לְךָ (2 Chron. 25.16) has a *patah* in the non-pausal imperative
masc. sing. [and חֲדָל (Jer. 40.4) with a *qames* in pause], the
patah is changed to a *shewa* in the pl. — חִדְלוּ הרע (Isa. 1.16),
but in pause it reverts to *qames* — חֲדָלוּ[84] (Zech. 11.12). The
same is the case with the future tense (the imperfect), where the
vowel in the 2nd per. sing. is changed to a *shewa* in the non-
pausal pl., but it reverts to the original vowel in pause, as
תִּשְׁמֹר, תִּשְׁמְרוּ, תֵּלְכוּ (Lev. 19.19); also with a *sere*, as תֵּלֵךְ,
תֵּלְכוּ (ibid. 26.3), and with a *patah*, as תִּשְׁמַע [in pause תִּשְׁמָע
(Hab. 1.2)], תִּשְׁמְעוּ, תִּשְׁמָעוּ (Deut. 13.5). A similar reversion to
the original vowel takes place in the past tense (the perfect),
so with a *sere*, as יָרֵאתָ, יָרְאָה (Jer. 3.8—), יָרֵאָה (Gen. 18.15); also
with a *holem*, as וּנָפוֹץ הכדים (Judg. 7.19), נָפְצָה (Gen. 9.19),
נָפוֹצָה (Jer. 10.21), and with a *qames*, as הָיְתָה, הָיָה (Gen. 18.12),
הָיָתָה (Isa. 14.24). Likewise is the case in the past pl., as [מָלְאָ
(Ex. 40.34+), מָלְאוּ (Gen. 29.21+), מָלֵאוּ[85] (Isa. 1.15)].

Here is another lacuna, then the fragments resume with a
study of the change of the *shewa* to a vowel in pausal forms.
Instances of change to *segol* in nouns, as פְּרִי, פֶּרִי[86] (Ezek. 17.23);
לְעַבְדֶּךָ, עַבְדְּךָ (Ps. 119.49), etc., except עַבְדְּךָ (ibid. 65) and
יְמִינְךָ (ibid. 110.5) which have a *shewa* in pause. Also in verbs,
as וַיְהִי, וַיֶּהִי (Ps. 33.9); יִסְעָדֶךָ (ibid. 20.3), וְנַעֲבְדֶךָ (1 Sam. 11.1),
etc. As for the rules of לך and בך, they are as follows: if they
are feminine, the *lamed* and *bet* are invariably vocalized with a
qames, whether pausal or non-pausal, as והקימותי לָךְ (Ezek.
16.60), ישתחווּ־לָךְ (Isa. 49.23). The same is the case in Aramaic,
they are always with a *qames*, as לָךְ (Dan. 2.23, 37), בָּךְ (ibid.

---

[84] *Miklol*, 16a.

[85] Quotations supplied conjecturally.

[86] *Ibid.*, 174a; *Halikot Sheva*, 40.

4.15, Targum Ex. 7.29). But if they are masculine, the *lamed* and *bet* have a *shewa* in non-pausal forms, as לְךָ נתתיה (Gen. 23.11), בְּךָ בטחתי (Ps. 25.2), and a *qameṣ* in pause, as נתתי לָךְ (Gen. 23.11), חסיתי בָךְ[87] (Ps. 16.1).

The part concludes with the rules of אתך and עמך. If they are feminine, the *taw* and *mem* have in all instances a *qameṣ*, as עִמָּךְ (Gen. 30.15, 2 Sam. 13.20), except מֵאִתָּךְ (Isa. 54.10) with a *ṣere*; in the masculine they have a *shewa* in non-pausal forms and a *qameṣ* in pause. So in ועשינו עִמָּךְ חסד of Josh. 2.14 the *kaf* has a *shewa* because עמך is feminine, but in Judg. 1.24 the *kaf* has a *qameṣ* because it is masculine.[88]

VII. The Non-Laryngeals and Laryngeals

Saadia treats in this part of the changes that take place in the vocalization of the laryngeal ע ח ה א and also ר as compared to that of the non-laryngeal consonants, especially in the vocalization of the prefixes and particles which are added to them. In view of the circumstance that the most important difference of

<hr>

[87] *Jāmiʿ al-Alfāẓ*, I, 222, 9 ff.; II, 79, 48 ff.; 164, 5 ff.; *Miklol*, 194a.

[88] *Ibid.*, 26a, 189a and 193b. At the end of this part it may be of interest to note the striking similarity of the rules regards the *shewa* given by Saadia here with those of Ḥayyūj in his *Sefer ha-Niqqud*, שער השוא הנע והנח (Dukes, 200 ff.; Nutt, 130 f.), a similarity extending to some of the same examples which include even the comparison of לשיזבותנא, error for ישיזבנך (Dan. 6.17), with ישיזבנכון (*ibid.*, 3.15). One can hardly escape the conclusion of Saadia's influence on Ḥayyūj in the latter's study of the *shewa*. Yet Ibn Janāḥ mentions twice the Gaon's reference to his Hebrew Grammar in the Commentary to *Sefer Yeṣirah*, then adds that he never saw it, neither did it reach Spain, *Lumaʿ*, 29, 2 ff.: וקד אשאר רב סעדיה רצّי אללה ענה אליْ דכר שי מנה (אחהע) פי שרחה לספר יצירה יחכי הנאלך אן לה פי דלך וצّעא נّאמעא ולם נרה נחן ולא וצל אלי בלדנא, also *ibid.*, 170, 4 ff. It is very likely that Saadia's Grammar was brought to Cordova by Dunash, Saadia's pupil, and it was probably used later by Ḥayyūj, also in Cordova, but some decades later, during the period of Ibn Janāḥ, it was no longer extant in Spain, or in Cordova, where Ibn Janāḥ resided, too.

the laryngeals from other consonants is that the former do not take a *dagesh*, much of the discussion here is to some extent a repetition of a number of points brought out in in Part IV treating of the *dagesh* and *rafe*.

He begins his study with a discussion of forms similar in their consonantal make up but differing in their vocalization or in the addition or omission of a consonant. So Saadia discusses the change that takes place in a verbal form by adding a *dagesh* in one of its radicals, as קָבַץ (1 Kings 20.1) and קִבֵּץ (cf. Deut. 30.3), or in its suffix, as יוֹרֶנּוּ (Isa. 28.26) וַיּוֹרֵנוּ (ibid. 2.3), or תַּעֲלֶנָה (Dan. 8.8) and לְי״י תַּעֲלֶנָה (Judg. 13.16), and like instances where the consonants in the words are the same, but the addition of a *dagesh* changes their respective meanings.[89] A similar change in meaning occurs with a change in the vocalization, as נִשְׁמַע (Josh. 1.17, Jer. 9.18) with a *patah* is the non-pausal form of the imperfect 1st p. pl. and of the participle of *nif'al*, but נִשְׁמָע (Josh. 24.24, Jer. 31.14 (15)) with a *qames* is the pausal of the same forms; also the change from *qames* to *shewa*, as שָׁמַע and שְׁמַע, or אָמַרְתָּ and אָמַרְתְּ, etc.

Here is a lacuna in the Ms. It resumes with a discussion of the vocalization of the prefixes ת נ י א in the imperfect before the laryngeals. This is followed by an extensive study of the seven particles שׁ מ ל כ ו ה ב. Saadia sets forth their functions as follows: The *bet* serves to express *cause* and *explanation* (ללעלה ואלתביין); the *he* — *affirmation* and *negation* (ללאתבאת ואלאנפא — definite and interrogative particles); the *waw* — *conjunction* (אלנסק״ה); the *kaf* — *comparison* (אלמתאל״ה); the *mem* — *acquisition* (אלאקתבאס״ה); the *lamed* — *purpose, aim* of an action (אלקצ״ה), and the *shin* — *relation* (אללד״ה[90]). Of

---

[89] These forms were previously discussed in Part IV, see *Proceedings*, XXI, 93 ff. [19 ff.].

[90] The functions and vocalization of these particles are discussed at length in *Jāmi' al-Alfāz* in the introductions to the respective parts of these

36   SAADIA GAON, THE EARLIEST HEBREW GRAMMARIAN

these particles, ל כ ב have the same vocalization, but the remaining ש מ ו ה are each one differently vocalized.

So ל כ ב are vocalized with a *patah* followed by a *dagesh* when prefixed to definite nouns beginning with a non-laryngeal, no matter whether the latter has a vowel or a *shewa*, as בַּלֶּחֶם (Gen. 47.17), בַּכְּבָשִׂים (Num. 15.11). But before not definite nouns these particles have a *shewa* if the former begin with a vocalized consonant and a *hireq* if they begin with a *shewa*, as בְּמֶלֶךְ (ibid. 21.26), בִּפְלַגּוֹת (Judg. 5.15). Before nouns beginning with a laryngeal, if they are bi-consonantal and definite, these particles take a *qames* before ע ה א and a *patah* before ח, as בָּעִיר (Gen. 19.12), בָּהָר (ibid. 19.30), בַּחֵיק (Prov. 16.33). If the nouns are tri-consonantal and not determinate, the three particles have a *shewa* before a laryngeal with a full vowel, as בְּחֶברוֹן, בְּאֶרֶץ (Gen. 13.18), and a *patah* before one without a full vowel (*hatef*), בַּהֲפֹךְ, בַּאֲשֶׁר (Gen. 19.29), with two exceptions where a *bet* has a *patah* before an 'ayin with a *shewa*: בַּעְרָב[91] (Isa. 21.13) and בַּעְשׂוֹת[92] (Ezek. 23.21). If these nouns are definite, the particles take a *qames* before ע ה א with a *shewa* (*hatef*) or with a vowel other than a qames, as בָּעֲנָקִים (Josh. 14.15), בָּאֲנָשִׁים (Deut. 1.35), בָּעֶרֶב (Gen. 19.1), except an 'ayin with *a holem* and a *he* with any vowel, in which cases the particles take a *patah*, as בַּעֲשֶׁק (Ezek. 22.7), בָּעֲרְבִים (Prov. 22.26), בַּהֵיכל (2 Chron. 4.7); if the laryngeals have a *qames* and are not tone-bearing, the prefixed particles take a *segol*, as בֶּעָרִים (Gen. 41.35), בֶּהָרִים (Ex. 32.12), except an *alef*, in which case the particles take a *qames*, as בָּאָרוֹן (Gen. 50.26); however, if the laryngeals are tone-bearing, such nouns are treated as bi-radicals. In the case of verbal nouns the particles take a *sere* when ac-

consonants see also *Luma'*, Chap. V, under the respective particles; *Sahot*, 15a ff.; *Miklol*, 42b ff., and Profiat Duran, *Ma'aseh Efod*, Chap. XIII.

[91] See *Minhat Shai* and Baer's note, *ad loc.*

[92] See *Minhat Shai* and Ginsburg's note, *ad loc.*

companied by a *meteg* (איקאף אלכלמה), as בֶּהָרֵג (Ezek. 26.15),
בְּעָטֵף[93] (Lam. 2.11).

As for definite nouns beginning with *ḥet*, if it has no full vowel
(גיר דאת נחו), the three particles take a *pataḥ*, as לַחֲכָמִים
(Ex. 7.11), כַּחֲלָלִים (Jer. 48.36); if it has a full vowel (דאת נחו)[94]
and it is *qameṣ*, the particles take a *segol*, as בֶּחָרָבָה (Gen. 7.22),
בֶּחֳדָשִׁים (Ezek. 45.17), בֶּחֳרָבוֹת (ibid. 33.27), but if the *ḥet* has
any of the other six vowels, the particles take a *pataḥ*, as בַּחֵמָר
(Ex. 2.3), בַּחַלּוֹן (Josh. 2.18), except two instances of בֶּחֳרָבוֹת
(Isa. 48.21, Ezek. 13.4), where the *bet* has a *qameṣ*.[95]

When the particles ל כ ב are prefixed to nouns beginning
with a *resh*, whether they are bi-consonantal or tri-consonantal,
if they are determined the particles usually take a *qameṣ*, as
בָּרָעָב (Gen. 41.36), בָּרְפָתִים (Hab. 3.17); in not determined
nouns, if the *resh* has a vowel, the particles take a *shewa*, as
בְּרֹאשָׁם (Lev. 21.5), בְּרוּחַ (Ex. 14.21), but if the former has a
shewa, the particles take a *ḥireq*, as בִּרְאוֹת (1 Chron. 21.28),
בִּרְכָלְתְּךָ (Ezek. 28.5).

When these particles are prefixed to an *alef* with a [*ḥaṭef*] *segol*
and they have no *meteg* on them, the *alef* becomes quiescent,
as בֵּאלֹהִים (Gen. 21.23), כֵּאלֹהִים[95a] (ibid. 3.5). When a *waw* is
added to the particle *bet*, it is pronounced אוּ, no matter whether
the *bet* has a vowel or a *shewa*, as וברב (Ex. 15.7), וּבְלָק[96] (Num.
22.4). But when it is added to the particles *kaf* [and *lamed*], it
is likewise pronounced אוּ if they have a *shewa* and takes a *shewa*
if the particles have a vowel.

---

[93] Cf. *Lumaʿ*, 263, 24, and 309, 20 f.; Ibn Ezra's Com. on Lam. 2.11;
Qimḥi's Com. on Ezek. 26.15 and *Miklol*, 54b, 56b f.

[94] So Ms., though some of the examples cited begin with a *ḥaṭef qameṣ*.

[95] Cf. *Miklol*, 158b; אכלה ואכלה, No. 25; *Massora Magna*, ed. Frensdorff,
70 b; *Minḥat Shai* on Ezek. 13.4.

[95a] Cf. *Miklol*, 39b.

[96] So Ms., although the *bet* in ובלק is not a particle, but the example was
evidently used because the rule applies to it just the same.

Here is a lacuna in the Ms., which resumes with the end of the discussion of some functions of the *waw*. This is followed by a study of the particle *lamed*, similar to that of *bet* and *kaf*. Saadia treats these three particles separately, although he stated at the outset that their vocalization is alike. After this one-leaf fragment there is another lacuna. The sections treating of the *he* as definite article and interrogative are missing, the Ms. resuming in the middle of Section 3 which treats of the pre-formative *he* in *hif'il*, *hof'al*, and *nif'al* forms, the first being active (אלאכתיאר, free choice of action) and the other two — passive (אלאצטראר, compulsive action).

So a *he* prefixed to [the infinitive of] active verbs beginning with a non-laryngeal takes a *patah* followed by *rafe*, as הַפְּלֵא (Isa. 29.14), הַשְׁמֵד (ibid. 14.23); but in the passive it takes a *hireq* followed by a *dagesh*, as הֻנָּתֹן תֻּנַּן (Jer. 38.3), הִקָּבְדִי (Ezek. 39.13), except two instances where the *he* in verbal nouns is replaced by an *alef*: אַשְׁכֵּים (Jer. 25.3), הָאִדָּרֹשׁ[97] (Ezek. 14.3). Before laryngeals in bi-consonantal verbs the *he* takes a *qames* in the active, as הָחֵל (1 Sam. 3.12), הָאֵר (Ps. 80.20), and a *shureq* in the passive, as הוּחַל (Gen. 4.26), הוּעַד (Ex. 21.29). In tri-consonantal verbs the *he* takes a *patah* followed by a [*hatef*] *patah* under the laryngeal, as הַחֲטִיא (Jer. 32.35), הֶעֱלוֹתִי (1 Sam. 8.8), except הַעְלֵם (Lev. 20.4) where the *'ayin* has a *shewa*; in the passive the *he* takes a *sere* and the laryngeal a *qames*, as הֵעָלוֹת (Num. 9.17), הֵעָשׂוֹתוֹ (Ezek. 43.13). The above rules apply largely to infinitives and imperatives.

The fourth section treats of the vocalization of the *he* in the perfect of *hif'il* forms. In bi-consonantal stems its vocalization occurs in three ways. (1) If the preformative *he* has a *qames* in the imperative, it is replaced by a *sere* in the perfect, as הָבֵא (Gen. 43.16) — הֵבִיא (ibid. 4.4). (2) If the *he* has a *patah* in the

---

[97] *Jāmi' al-Alfāz*, I, 439, 77 ff.; *Luma'*, 87, 12 ff.; *Ṣahot*, 13a; *Miklol*, 28b.

imperative, it is changed to a *hireq* in the perfect, as הֻכַּר (Gen. 31.32)—הֻכִּיר (Deut. 33.9), הֻכָּה (ibid. 13.16) — הֻכָּה (Ex. 9.25). (3) If the *he* has a *holem* in the imperative, it remains unchanged in the perfect, as הוליד (cf. Jer. 29.6) — הוליד (Gen. 11.27), הופיע (Ps. 94.1).

In tri-consonantal stems beginning with a non-laryngeal, if the preformative *he* has a *patah* in the imperative, it is changed to a *hireq* in the perfect, as הַקְרב (Ex. 28.1) — הִקְריב (Gen. 12.11). In stems beginning with a laryngeal the *he* takes likewise a *patah* in the imperative, followed by a [*hatef*] *patah* under the laryngeal (or a *shewa* under a non-laryngeal), and in the perfect the vowel of the *he* is changed to a segol, as הַחֲזֵק (2 Sam. 11.25) — הֶחֱזִיק (Judg. 7.8), הַעֲבָר־נָא (2 Sam. 24.10) — [הֶעֱבִיר (Gen. 47.21)].

The vocalization of the *waw* copulative (אלוו אלנסקּיّה) takes place in five ways: *shewa, patah, qames, shureq,* and *hireq,* depending on whether it is prefixed to the laryngeals ע ה ח א, to the labials פ מ ו ב, or the remaining 14 consonants. (1) Before a word beginning with one of the 14 consonants with a vowel the *waw* takes a *shewa,* as וְדָרְשׁוּ (Deut. 19.18), but if the consonant has a *shewa,* the *waw* takes a *shureq,* as וּגְבחים (Eccl. 5.7). (2) Before a word beginning with a laryngeal with a full vowel the *waw* takes a *shewa,* as וְהַמִּצְפֶּה (Gen. 31.49), but if the former has a *shewa* (*hatef*), the *waw* takes a *patah,* as וַאֲמרתם (ibid. 32.21). [98] וְנֶהֱלכתם (ibid. 19.2). (3) Before a labial the *waw* is invariably vocalized with a *shureq,* no matter whether the labial has a vowel or a *shewa,* as וּבֵן (Num. 27.8), וּבְני (1 Sam. 9.16). This rule also applies to nouns beginning with a *waw,* as וָלֹד (Gen. 11.30), וָהֵב (Num. 21.14), though such nouns are not found in the Bible with a *waw* copulative. The above-

---

[98] The vocalization of the *waw* before a laryngeal with a *hatef qames* or *hatef segol* is not mentioned.

mentioned rules govern both bi-consonantal and tri-consonantal
words.

Exceptions from these rules are nouns in pause which have the
tone on the first consonant, in which case the *waw* copulative
takes a *qameṣ*, no matter whether the nouns begin with a non-
laryngeal, a laryngeal, or a labial. So the non-pausal וּמֵת (Ex.
11.5) is וָמֵת (Gen. 44.31) in pause, וְעֵץ הַחיים (ibid. 2.9) — וָעֵץ
(1 Chron. 22.15 (14)) in pause, וְחֶבֶר הוֹלִיד (ibid. 7.32) — וָחֶבֶר
(ibid. 8.17), וְקֶצֶף גדול (Zech. 1.15) — וָקֶצֶף[99] (Eccl. 5.16), etc.,
except two instances of the *waw* with a *qameṣ* in non-pausal
nouns: וָפֶרֶץ וזרח (Gen. 46.12) and פִיתון וָמֶלֶךְ[100] (1 Chron. 8.35).

Finally, there are four forms where the *waw* copulative takes
a *ḥireq*:[101] וְהִיוּ (1 Sam. 4.9), וִהְיִיתֶם (Gen. 3.5), וִחְיוּ (ibid. 42.18),
and וִחְיִיתֶם (Ezek. 37.5). Apart from these and the two exceptions mentioned above the *waw* copulative in non-pausal forms
takes a *pataḥ* before laryngeals, a *shureq* before labials, and a
shewa before the 14 other consonants.[102]

The particle *mem* serves most frequently to denote *acquisition*
(אלאקתבאסֿיֿה),[103] but occasionally also to indicate *lending*
(אעאריֿה?),[104] and it is prefixed to some participles, too. Its

---

[99] *Ṣaḥot*, 21b; *Miklol*, 49b f.

[100] See *Massora Magna*, 112a, 316a, and references given there.

[101] The Ms. has here אלכפֿץ אלאצגר, a term usually employed by Saadia
to denote a *ṣere*. Elsewhere he is wont to designate a *ḥireq* אלכפֿץ אלאכבר,
see p. 47, below.

[102] Omitting the rule that the *waw* takes a *shureq* before these consonants
with a *shewa*. See *Jāmiʿ al-Alfāẓ*, I, 457 ff., for a comprehensive study of the
various uses and vocalization of the *waw*; cf. also *Kitāb al-Lin*, 15, 16 ff.;
49, 24 ff.; *Ṣaḥot*, 21b ff.; *Miklol*, 48b ff., and *Maʿaseh Efod*, 74 ff.

[103] The usual meaning of الاقتباس is *acquisition of knowledge* (also seeking
or acquiring fire); as technical term, it means *a quotation*, as from the Koran
or Ḥadīth, see Jurjānī, *Taʿrīfāt*, s. v.; *Muḥiṭ*, 1653b; also Reckendorf, *Arab.
Syntax*, p. 390, 4.

[104] The Ms. reads here וקד וחﮩﮐ תכון איעאריֿה, but later it is referred to
as ללאעאדֿה, *repetition*, which would hardly fit here. I read it, therefore,

vocalization in the first two cases occurs in two ways: when added (1) to the laryngeals and *resh*, and (2) to the remaining 17 consonants. In the latter case the *mem* takes in all instances a *ḥireq*, followed by a *dagesh* in the consonant to which it is prefixed, as, e. g., מִנַּעֲרתךָ (Ps. 18.16), מִזְּבֻל לוֹ (ibid. 49.15), מִיְרֻשָּׁתְךָ (2 Chron. 20.11), except the two instances: מְלָאם (Gen. 25.23) and מִנְבוּרתם[105] (Ezek. 32.30), where the consonants to which the *mem* is added are *rafe*. Prefixed to words beginning with a laryngeal or *resh*, the *mem* takes invariably a *ṣere* followed by a *rafe*, as, e. g., וּמֵאֲצִילֶיהָ (Isa. 41.9), וּמֵהֲרָיוֹן (Hos. 9.11), except וּמִן רָגְזֶךָ (Isa. 14.3) where the *mem* has a *ḥireq* before a *resh*.[106]

The *mem* prefixed to participles of tri-consonantal verbs takes a *pataḥ* in the active, as מַקְרִיב (Lev. 3.1), מַעֲבִיר (Deut. 18.10), and a *shureq* in the passive, as מְקֹרח (Ezek. 29.18), מְקְטֹר (Mal. 1.11). In participial forms of bi-consonantal verbs the vocalization of the *mem* varies. At times it is a *ḥolem*, as מוֹצִיא (Ps. 68.7), or a *ṣere*, as מֵפֵר (Isa. 44.25), מֵשִׁיב (Gen. 20.7+), or a *pataḥ* followed by a *dagesh*, as מַכֶּה (Ex. 2.11), מַצִּיל (Deut. 32.39+), etc., each in accordance with its particular form, as has been previously explained in connection with the prefixes תניא, similar to the vocalization of the prefixed *he* in verbal forms.[107]

Among the eleven servile consonants the *shin* is employed as prefix the least. Added to a word beginning with one of the 18 non-laryngeals, including the *resh*, the *shin* takes a *segol* followed by a *dagesh*, as שֶׁשְּׁזָפַתְנִי (Cant. 1.6), שֶׁתֶּחְפַּץ (ibid. 2.7), שֶׁשָּׁם

אעאריה (=עאריה), *borrowing* or *lending*. Unfortunately, the unique Ms. is very faulty, and it is difficult at times to reconstruct the correct text.

[105] See *Proceedings*, XXI, 94 [20], n. 50.

[106] Cf. *Jāmiʿ al-Alfāẓ*, II, 180, 10, for a number of instances of *mem* with a *ḥireq* before laryngeals and *resh*; see Qimḥi on Isa. 14.3, *Miklol*, 48a, and his *Shorashim*, s. v. רגז.

[107] See pp. 31 f., above.

(Ps. 122.4), שֶׁיָּבוֹא (Eccl. 2.12), and with a *resh*: שֶׁרֹאשִׁי (Cant. 5.2). Prefixed to a laryngeal, the *shin* takes likewise a *segol*, but is not followed by a *dagesh*, as שֶׁיָּי אלהיו (Ps. 144.15), שֶׁאַנִּיחֶנּו (Eccl. 2.18), שֶׁהֱבֵיאתִיו (Cant. 3.4), except שֶׁהֵם בהמה (Eccl. 3.18) which has a *shewa*.[108] The *shin* is most frequently used as particle in Ecclesiastes and the Song of Songs.

This concludes the study of the seven particles שׁ מ ל כ ו ה ב which comprise, together with תּ נ י א, the eleven servile consonants אבהו יכל מנשת, for the remaining eleven גד זח טסע פץ קר may serve as radicals only.[109]

It should be mentioned here that a brief summary of the rules discussed in this part, especially those applied to the laryngeals and the labials, is given by Saadia in his Commentary on *Sefer Yeṣirah*.[110] He mentions there the 42 rules peculiar to ע ח ה א, 17 of which are common to the reading of the Babylonians and Palestinians, while the remaining 25 are followed only by the Palestinians. He also states that he devoted a separate part of "Kutub al-Lughah" to the study of these 42 peculiarities. While this number is not mentioned in the preserved fragments of this part, there is little doubt that it is the one to which he refers, as seen from his introductory remarks to Part VIII which follows, where this number is mentioned.

VIII. THE LARYNGEALS

Saadia begins his study of the laryngeals ע ח ה א with a reference to the 50 rules characteristic of them. 42 of these rules have already been discussed in relation to the eleven servile

---

[108] Cf. *Jāmiʿ al-Alfāẓ*, II, 634, 4 ff.; *Lumaʿ*, 36, 19 ff.; *Ṣaḥot*, 31b; *Zikkaron*, 7; *Miklol*, 42a f.

[109] See *Proceedings*, XXI, 81 [7].

[110] *Commentaire*, 76, 2,—78, last line. See Harkavy's tabulation in *Zikron*, V, 61 ff., and Bacher, *Anfänge*, 42 ff.

consonants אבהו יכל מנשת, which was the main subject of study
of Part VII. The remaining eight rules peculiar to the laryngeals
have no relation to the servile consonants, so they are discussed
here separately, as follows.

(1) The intensive form of tri-consonantal verbs, whether
active or passive (*pi'el* or *pu'al*),[111] must always have a *dagesh*
in the middle radical if it is a non-laryngeal and not a *resh*; so,
e. g., אֲשַׁלַּח (Gen. 38.17), אֲקַבֵּץ (Isa. 56.8), and with objective
suffixes אֲשַׁלֵּחֶךָ (Gen. 32.27), אֲקַבְּצֶךָ (Isa. 43.5), and in
the passive שֻׁלַּחְתִּי (Dan. 10.11), עֻשֵּׂיתִי (Ps. 139.15), רֻקַּמְתִּי
(ibid.). But if the middle radical is a laryngeal or a *resh*, it does
not take a *dagesh*, as אֲנַהֵל (cf. Isa. 40.11), ארחם (Ex. 33.19),
קֵרַבְתִּי (Isa. 46.13), נֶאֶרְתָה (Ps. 89.40); מְקֻטֶּרֶת (Cant. 3.6) with
a non-laryngeal, מְפֹרָצֶת (Nehem. 1.3) with a *resh*.[112] Saadia
gives no explanation for the vocalic changes in forms like קרבתי,
מפרצת, נארתה.

(2) In tri-consonantal verbs which have the form of "*qames*
and *patah*" in the past (*qal*), as שָׁמַע, and in the pl. שָׁמְעוּ, if the
middle radical is a non-laryngeal the usual change to the imperative masc. pl. is a *hireq* under the first radical, as שִׁמְעוּ, but if it
is a laryngeal (but not a *resh*) it is changed to a *patah*. So שָׁאֲלוּ
לֶחֶם (Lam. 4.4) is שַׁאֲלוּ (Jer. 18.13) in the imperative, וְשָׁחֲטוּ
(Ex. 12.6) — וְשָׁחֲטוּ[113] (ibid. 21).

(3) In segolates like מֶלֶךְ, פֶּרֶד, if the first radical is a laryngeal
the vocalization remains unchanged, as חֶבֶר (Hos. 6.9), אדר
(Micah 2.8); however, if the second radical is a laryngeal both
vowels are changed to *patah*s, as נַחַל (Num. 13.23), בעל (Gen.
37.19), נהם (Prov. 19.12), but if the third is a laryngeal, only

<hr>

[111] These terms are not used by Saadia, instead he describes these
conjugations by such phrases as פאעל ומפעול באצטראר and פעל בקהר,
all the illustrative examples belonging to *pi'el* and *pu'al*.

[112] *Commentaire*, 77, last line ff.

[113] *Ibid.*, 78, 2 ff. Cf. *Miklol*, 15b f.

44   SAADIA GAON, THE EARLIEST HEBREW GRAMMARIAN

the second vowel is changed to *patah*, as זֶרַע (Gen. 1.11), זבח[114] (ibid. 31.54). All such segolates follow this rule except לֶחֶם and רֶחֶם (Gen. 20.18) which remain unchanged, though the middle radical is a laryngeal.[115]

(4) In tri-consonantal nouns vocalized with *holem* and *segol*, as אֹכֶל (Gen. 41.35), אֹמֶץ (Job 17.9), if the second or the third radical is a laryngeal the *segol* changes to a *patah*, as גֹּעַל (cf. Ezek. 16.5), בֹּחַן (Isa. 28.16), גבה (Ezek. 41.8), נכח[116] (Ex. 26.35).

(5) The fem. participle of tri-consonantal verbs is vocalized in non-laryngeals with two *segols*, as אֹמֶרֶת (1 Kings 3.22), הָעֹזֶבֶת (Prov. 2.17), מתאַמֶּצֶת (Ruth 1.8), מתרפקת (Cant. 8.5), but if the third radical is a laryngeal the *segols* change to *patahs*, as שֹׁמַעַת (Gen. 18.10), סֹרַחַת (Ezek. 17.6), מתלַקַּחַת (Ex. 9.24); also מַרְחֶשֶׁת (Lev. 2.7) and מִשְׁלַחַת (Ps. 78.49), and likewise in bi-radical stems, as לָגַעַת בך[117] (2 Sam. 14.10).

(6) The text of the two-leaf fragment of this part ends abruptly in the beginning of this rule with a lacuna in the Ms., but it could be supplemented from Saadia's summary in his Commentary on *Sefer Yeṣirah*, as follows: In infinitives of tri-consonantal verbs where the second radical has a *holem* and the third — a *shewa* with a non-laryngeal, as לִשְׁמֹר, the *shewa* changes to a *patah* with a laryngeal, as לִפְקֹחַ (Isa. 42.7), לשמע.[118] From the same summary could be in all likelihood reconstructed the remaining two rules, briefly stated in the following terms.

(7) In participles masc. sing. of tri-consonantal verbs, if the third radical is a laryngeal following a *ṣere*, it takes a *patah*, as שֹׁמֵעַ, זֹורֵחַ[119] (Eccl. 1.5).

---

[114] *Commentaire*, 78, 9 ff. Cf. *Luma‘*, 107, 2 f.; *Zikkaron*, 22, 14 ff.; *Miklol*, 150b f.

[115] *Ibid.*, 151a.

[116] *Commentaire*, 78, 12. Cf. *Zikkaron*, 23, 3; *Miklol*, 143b f.

[117] *Commentaire*, 78, 13 f. Cf. *Miklol* 12a, 73b.

[118] *Commentaire*, 78, 14 f.   [119] *Ibid.*, 16. Cf. *Miklol*, 9a f.

(8) Similarly when the third radical is a laryngeal following a *hireq* or a *shureq*, it takes a *patah*, as יוֹשִׁיעַ (Isa. 45.20), יַצְלִיחַ (Ps. 1.3), סָרוּחַ (Ex. 26.13), יהושע.[120]

Thus, one can readily see that a rather brief summary of the eight rules pertaining the laryngeals discussed in this part was likewise included in the above mentioned Commentary.

IX. The Expletives and Affixes

There remains a four-leaf fragment in the Leningrad Ms., which contains a study of the so called "added" consonants (אלזואיד), or expletives, in the middle and at the end of the word, as well as a discussion of some phases of the affixes (אללואחק). The fragment has no beginning nor end of the discussion and appears to belong to a separate part treating of expletives and affixes, most likely Part IX.

It starts in the middle of the study of the expletive *he*. It occurs in nouns[120a] with pronominal suffixes, as שמועה, in the pl. שמועות, and with pron. suffix of 3rd per. masc. pl. it could be both שמועותם and שמועותיהם, by analogy with נפשותם (cf. Num. 17.3), נפשותיהם (Ex. 16.16), and in the latter instance the *he* is pleonastic. In verbs the expletive *he* occurs in 3 ways: (1) In objective suffixes of 3rd per. masc. sing., for one may say יִצְרוֹ (cf. תִּתְּנוֹ Ex. 22.29), יִצְּרֶהוּ, or יִצְּרֶנְהוּ (Deut. 32.10), וכפרתהו (Ezek. 43.20). (2) In suffixes of 3rd per masc. pl., as יביאם (Num. 27.17), יְבִיאֵהֶם, by analogy with אפאיהם, אפאם[121] (Deut. 32.26). (3) Suffixes of 3rd per. fem. pl., as תשמיען, תשמיעהן, evidently by the same analogy.

---

[120] *Commentaire*, 78, 16 f. Cf. *Miklol*, 13a.

[120a] Saadia refers to nouns, as שמועה, and later also to participles, as עושה, by נעת, pl. נעות, a term usually applied to adjectives, qualifications.

[121] Cf. *Jāmi' al-Alfāẓ*, II, 444, 18 ff.; *Mahberet*, 140a; *Kitāb al-Līn*, 198, 7;

The second expletive in the middle of the word is a *mem*, usually followed by *waw*, which are added to the 4 servile consonants: מ ל כ ב. So במו אש (Isa. 43.2) =באש; כמו אפל (Job 10.22) =כאפל, כמוכם (ibid. 12.3) =ככם, כמוהם (Judg. 8.18) = כהם[122] (with the exception of כמו in כמוכם and כמוהם, it is a separate word); למו חרב (Job 27.14) =לחרב; similar constructions may be made also with a *mem*, as ממו ספר, ממו אש, although they do not occur in the Bible.

The third expletive in the middle of the word is a *nun*, and it occurs both in nouns and in verbs. In nouns, as עוֹשָׂי (Job 35.10) and עֲשָׂנִי (ibid. 31.15), בְּשׁוּבִי (Judg. 8.9) and בְּשׁוּבֶנִי[123] (Ezek. 47.7), the meaning in both instances being the same. In verbs it occurs in three ways: (1) In objective suffixes of 3rd per. masc. sing., as יִבְנֶנּוּ (Nehem. 3.14) and יִבְנֶהוּ (Job 20.19), וילכדֵהוּ (2 Chron. 22.9) and ילכדֶנּוּ (Prov. 5.22). (2) In suffixes of 3rd per. fem. sing., as ימצאֶהָ (cf. Gen. 16.7) and ימצאֶנה (cf. Jer. 2.24). (3) In suffixes of 3rd per. masc. pl., as מהם and מנהם (Job 11.20), ישמעום and ישמעונהם (cf. יעברנהו Jer. 5.22). Thus, the four formations יָצְרוֹ (cf. תִּתְּנוֹ Ex. 22.29), יִצְרֶנּוּ (cf. Ps. 12.8), [יִצְרֶנְהוּ (Deut. 32.10)], and יִנְצְרֶהוּ (cf. Ps. 61.8) have the same signification.[124]

The fourth expletive in the middle of the word is a *taw*, and it occurs in two ways: (1) between the preformative and the stem, and (2) between stem and the afformative. In the latter case it occurs only in fem. nouns, as ישועה (Isa. 26.1) and ישועתה (Jonah 2.10), המות and הַמָּוְתָה (Ps. 116.15), etc., where the *taw* does not add anything to the primary meaning of the

---

Luma', 147, 16 f.; *Miklol*, 34b. Cf. also Targum, Rashi, Ibn Ezra, Nahmanides, and Aaron Niqomodio, *Keter Torah*, on Deut. 32.26.

[122] Cf. *Jāmi' al-Alfāz*, II, 110, 9 ff.

[123] Cf. *Luma'*, 200, 23 ff.; *Sahot*, 29b; *Miklol*, 29b, 33a.

[124] Cf. *Jāmi' al-Alfāz*, II, 243, 61 ff.; *Luma'*, 73, 3 ff.; 197, 20 ff.; 198, 7 ff.; *Sahot*, 20a; *Miklol*, 35b.

words.[125] The *taw* between the preformative and the stem occurs only in passive (*hitpa'el*),[126] and it comes in four different ways: (a) preceding the stem, (b) infixed in the stem, (c) changed into another consonant, and (d) dropped altogether. The *taw* precedes the stem when the latter begins with one of the following 16 consonants: ר ק פ ע נ מ ל כ י ח ו ה ד ג ב א, as מתאמצת (Ruth 1.18), המתברך (Isa. 65.16), etc.[127] In stems beginning with ס and שׁ the *taw* is infixed after these consonants, as ויסתבל (Eccl. 12.5), מהשתרע (Isa. 28.20), ישתרגו (Lam. 1.14), etc., except והתשוטטנה (Jer. 49.3), as was explained in connection with משתמע.[128] The *taw* changes into ד after a ז, as הִזְדַּמִּנְתּוּן (Dan. 2.9) in the Aramaic and נזדמן לו רוק (Berakot 24b) in New Hebrew, and into ט after a צ, as וַיִּצְטַיָּרוּ (Josh. 9.4), הִצְטַיַּדְנוּ (ibid. 12). It is dropped before stems beginning with ט, as מִטַּהֲרִים (Nehem. 13.22), הִטֶּהָרוּ (Ezra 6.20), and with ת, as תִּתַּמָּם (2 Sam. 22.26), וַנִּתְתָּפֵשׂ[129] (Jer. 51.41).

Expletives at the end of the word are three: ה, ו, and י. The expletive *he* occurs in three ways: (1) In the imperative, as שְׁמַע (Gen. 21.12 — שִׁמְעָה (Ps. 17.1), הַקְשִׁיבָה (Jer. 18.19). and in the imperfect 1st per. sing. and pl., as אֶעְבְּרָה (Num. 21.22), אָשׁוּבָה (Gen. 30.31), נָבוֹאָה (Ps. 132.7), נלכה (Gen. 22.5), also יוצִיאה, יבואה (the cohortative *he*); in all such instances the *he* is adjacent

---

[125] Cf. *Jāmi' al-Alfāẓ*, I, 78, 140 ff., where אלה י should be read ו אלת, as seen in II, 715, 33 ff.; *Luma'*, 80, 22 ff.; 266, 22 f.

[126] The implication evidently is that the verb could be a passive without a *taw*, a *pu'al*, it could therefore, be considered pleonastic, for Saadia takes the *hitpa'el* form as a passive (אלאצטראר), not a reflexive.

[127] Saadia cites examples before each of the 16 consonants, consecutively.

[128] Unfortunately, this study is missing in the fragments so far identified. On והתשוטטנה see *Mustalḥaq*, 137; Ibn Bal'am and Qimḥi *ad loc.*; *Ṣaḥot*, 67a; *Moznayim*, 16b; *Miklol*, 70a.

[129] The idea of assimilation of one consonant to another was unknown to Saadia. Cf. *Jāmi' al-Alfāẓ*, I, 490, 24 ff.; *Mustalḥaq*, 129 ff.; Ibn Bal'am on Isa. 1.6 and Jer. 49.3; *Ṣaḥot*, 17a, 67a; *Moznayim*, 23a; *Miklol*, 68a f., 69a ff.

to the stem.[130] (2) When there is another servile consonant between the stem and the *he*, as לָהֵמָה (Jer. 14.16), בהמה (Ex. 30-4); also בְּתוֹכֵהֶנָה (Ezek. 16.53). לְכָלֵהֶנָה[131] (1 Kings 7.37), תִּשָּׁמַעְנָה[132] (Isa. 30.21), בָּאָנָה (Jer. 8.7). In these two ways the *he* is preceded by a *qames*. (3) When the expletive *he* is preceded by a *sere*: מַלְאָכֵכָה[133] (Nah. 2.14).

The expletive *waw* occurs in singular and plural forms. In singular forms the *waw* is adjacent to the stem, as בְּנוֹ צִפֹּר (Num. 23.18), לְמֵעֵינוֹ[134] (Ps. 114.118). In plural forms there is a servile consonant between the stem and the *waw*, so if that consonant has *shureq* the *waw* takes likewise a *shureq*, as יְכַסְיֻמוּ (Ex. 15.5), but if it has any other vowel the *waw* takes a *holem*, as תְבִיאֵמוֹ (ibid. 17), כְּסָמוֹ (ibid. 10), גִרְשְׁתָּמוֹ[135] (ibid. 23.31).

The expletive *yod* may take either a *hireq* or a *sere*. It takes a *hireq* when adjoining the stem, as הַיוֹשְבִי (Ps. 123.1), הַמַגְבִיהִי[136] (ibid. 113.5), or when the *yod* is added to the pronominal suffix of 2nd per. fem. sing., as עֲוֹנֵכִי . . . תַחֲלוּאָיְכִי (ibid. 103.3), רְעָתֵכִי[137] (Jer. 11.15). The *yod* takes a *sere* when added to words such as עַד, עַל, אֶל, as אֱלֵי־מִים (Job 29.19), עֲלֵי־כֶסֶל (ibid. 15.20),

---

[130] Cf. *Jāmiʻ al-Alfāẓ*, I, 416, 38 ff., and elsewhere; *Mahberet*, 8a; *Ṣahot*, 19a; *Miklol*, 15a, 17b.

[131] Cf. *Lumaʻ*, 367, 17 ff.; *Ṣahot*, 20a; *Miklol*, 30a, 192b, 193b.

[132] Probably because this form occurs occasionally without a *he*, as e. g., in Gen. 19.33.

[133] Cf. *Jāmi al-Alfāẓ*, II, 210, 68; *Lumaʻ*, 80, 14 ff., 91, 1 f.; Ibn Ezra and Qimḥi, *ad loc.*; *Miklol*, 143b; for Ibn Balʻam explanation of מלאככה see Qimḥi, *Shorashim*, s. v. לאך; cf. Poznański, "Com. of Ibn Balʻam on the Minor Prophets," *JQR*, N. S., XV, 43, n. 7.

[134] See *Jāmiʻ al-Alfāẓ*, I, 465, 166 ff.; *Mahberet*, 75b f.; *Lumaʻ*, 55, 13 ff.; *Ṣahot*, 23a.

[135] *Jāmiʻ al-Alfāẓ*, loc. cit.; *Lumaʻ*, 97, 5; 194, 2 ff., 17 ff.; *Ṣahot*, 23a; *Moznayim*, 6a; *Miklol*, 26b, 144b f., 192b.

[136] Cf. *Jāmiʻ al-Alfāẓ*, II, 34, 158 ff.; *Lumaʻ*, 60, 11 ff.; *Ṣahot*, 26b; *Moznayim*, 7a; *Miklol*, 10a.

[137] Cf. *Lumaʻ*, 61, 1 f.; *Ṣahot*, 26b; *Miklol*, 144a, 145a.

עֲדֵי אֲבֹד[137a] (Num. 24.24). In all these instances the addition of the *yod* does not in any way change the meaning of the words.

Thus, the three expletives י ו ה occur only at the end of the word,[138] while the other three, ת נ מ, occur both in the middle and at the end of the word.

Here Saadia points out some deviations from the rules regarding tri-consonantal verbs he had previously discussed. So if there is a *dagesh* in the middle radical the verb becomes intensively transitive (אלפאעל פי גיר דׂאתה בקהר), as שִׁמְעוּ (cf. 1 Sam. 15.4); however, if the middle radical is one of the spirants ב ג ד כ פ ת and it has a *dagesh*, the verb is intransitive (פאעל פי דׂאתה), as דִּבְּרוּ, דִּבֶּר. Another deviation in these verbs is when the first radical is an *alef* or a *yod*, in which case the *alef* is silent in the imperfect of the intrasitive (*qal*), as יֹאכַל, אָכַל, and the waw (= *yod*) is silent in the imperfect of the transitive (*hif'il*), as נוֹלִיד, אוֹלִיד. Saadia calls attention to the fact that in verbs with the first radical a *yod* the prefix in the imperfect takes in some of them a *ḥireq* with the *yod* silent, as יִירַשׁ, אִירַשׁ, and in others it takes a *ṣere* (with the *yod* omitted), as אֵרֵד, אֵשֵׁב. He emphasizes that one should not look for any particular reason why in one case the prefix takes a *ḥireq* and in the other — a *ṣere*, for both the consonantal and the vocalic make up of a word originate in the conventional usage of the language. One should not, therefore, attempt finding a reason why, e. g., דָּבָר is with two *qameṣes*, נֶפֶשׁ — with two *segols*, and נַחַל — with two *pataḥs*,[138a] except that this vocalization was so accepted by linguistic usage.

[137a] *Ibid.*, 189b. Cf. *Jāmi' al-Alfāẓ*, II, 396, 21 f.

[138] But previously the *he* was mentioned by Saadia as the first of the expletives of the middle in the word.

[138a] But see p. 36, above, where Saadia gives the reason for the change

As for bi-radical verbs, such as שב, קם, since they have no third radical, their nominal construction is formed by the addition of a *he*, as קוֹמָה (1 Kings 7.35), שׁוּבָה (cf. Isa. 30.15), בִּיאָה (cf. בַּבִּאָה Ezek. 8.5 and ביאה in New Hebrew). In verbs the nominal forms of which begin with *mem* and end with *he*, as מראה, מעשה, these consonants are dropped in their inflection,[139] as וירא, וַיַּעַשׂ, so in some respects they become like bi-consonantal verbs.

The fragment ends abruptly in the beginning of a discussion of the eleven prefixes, of which four, ת נ י א, change the vocalization of the word to which they are prefixed.

Saadia seems to distinguish what he designates as augmentation, or amplification, of a stem (תפכים, or פיאור in medieval Hebrew), which is treated in Part II of "Kutub al-Lughah," from what he considers a pleonastic addition of consonants under various conditions, treated in this part. He usually refers to the latter as אלזואיד, "added" consonants, which comprise the servile consonants ת נ מ י ו ה, but in the case of תפכים, augmentation of the stem, it may occur with every consonant of the alphabet, as previously discussed in the second part. But he is not always consistent in this distinction; so, e. g., in his comment on מְלָוֹשְׁנִי (Ps. 101.5) he states that "the *yod* in this word is used as amplification, as in שֹׁכְנִי (Jer. 49.16), חֹקְקִי . . . חֹצְבִי[140] (Isa. 22.16)," the same examples given here as illustrations of the expletive *yod*.

---

in segolates from two *segols* to two *patahs*, as בַּעַל, נַחַל, because the second radical is a laryngeal.

[139] The inflection of such forms is discussed by Saadia in Part II, see *Proceedings*, XXI, 83, 9.

[140] *Sa'adja al-Fajjûmi's arab. Übers. u. Erklärung d. Psalmen*, ed. Eisen, Leipzig, 1934, 34, 16 f.: ואליוד פי אלכלמה (מלושני) תפכימא מתל שכני בחגוי סלע ומתל חצבי מרום קברו חקקי בסלע.

Dunash cites Saadia's rule regarding the expletive *mem* followed by a *waw*, as במורפי (Job 16.5) =בפי, למורפי (ibid. 40.4) = כמו אפל, לפי (ibid. 10.22) =כאפל.[141] Yet in the following paragraph Dunash cites a number of instances of so called added consonants, as in תגמולוהי (Ps. 116.12), יצרנהו (Deut. 32.10), וגרשתמו (Ex. 23.31), etc., as examples of emphatic amplifications (ומן המפואר),[142] the same and similar instances which the Gaon cites in this part as examples of expletives which do not in any way add or modify the meaning of the words.

David b. Abraham also refers to the various cases of expletives, discussed here by Saadia, as amplification (תפכים).[143] So is the case with the *he* in nouns like קוֹמָה (1 Kings 7.35), רוֹמָה[144] (Micah 2.3), or in the imperative, as קוּמָה י"י (Num. 10.35), שְׁמָעָה (Dan. 9.19), and in the imperfect, as אשמעה (Jer. 4.21), אזכרה (Ps. 42.5), (the cohortative *he*), etc. Other instances of amplification are the *waw* in בנו בער (Num. 24.3), למעינו מים (Ps. 114.8), תבָאֵמו ותטעמו (Ex. 15.17), יכסיֵמו (ibid. 5), etc.; the *yod* in מושיבי (Ps. 113.9), המשפילי (ibid. 6), etc., איך תשָקֹטי[145] (Jer. 47.7), עלי־עָשׂוֹר (Ps. 92.4), etc.; the *mem* in מרעים (Judg. 14.11), כַּשָׁנִים[146] (Isa. 1.18); the *nun* in יְסֹבְבֶנְהוּ (Deut. 32.10), בשׁוּבְנִי (Ezek. 47.7), and in Aramaic אנתון[147] (Dan. 2.8), and the *taw* in עֻוְלָתָה (Ezek. 28.15), ישועתה (Jonah 2.10), משתחויתם[148]

ודע כי כל מילה שתיכנס בתוך הדברים לא תוסיף[141] *Teshubot*, No. 109. בטעם כלום כמו אאמצכם במו פי (Job 16.5) טעמו בפי וגו'

[142] *Ibid.*, No. 110.

[143] The references to most of them were given above in connection with Saadia's discussion of the respective expletives.

[144] *Jāmiʻ al-Alfāẓ*, 1, 416, 36 ff.; see also *ibid.*, 415, 32 ff., that the *he* in forms like יהושיע (I Sam. 17.47), יהודוך (Ps. 45.18), ביהוסף (*ibid.* 81.6), etc., is likewise תפכים, a view maintained also by Dunash (*Teshubot*, No. 110).

[145] *Jāmiʻ al-Alfāẓ*, II, 34, 156 f.

[146] *Ibid.*, 182, 47 ff.; 689, 38 f.

[147] *Ibid.*, 243, 61 ff., also 67 f.: ולנא נון פי אואכר אלאלפאט פצאחחֿ ללעבראני ולים בזאיד פי אלמעני שיא

[148] *Ibid.*, 715, 29 f.

(Ezek. 8.16). In general, this Karaite lexicographer and grammarian is wont to explain various unusual or rare formation both in Hebrew and in Aramaic as תפכים, including the so called augmentation in stems, as ימחאו (Isa. 55.12), וְהֶאֱזְנִיחוּ[149] (ibid. 19.6), also וָעֳמָמִים (Nehem. 9.22), עַמְמַיָא[150] (Dan. 3.4).

X. Permutation

While the so far available text of Saadia Gaon's Grammar "Kutub al-Lughah" ends with the above-mentioned fragments, which comprise portions of eight parts out of the twelve of which it consisted, one should also mention here that Dunash refers to another part of this Grammar, which deals with permutation, or interchange of consonants (שער החילופים). He criticizes the Gaon's interpretation of וַתֵּלַהּ (Gen. 47.13) as וַתֶּלָא (Job 4.5), with the *alef* replaced by a *he*;[151] indeed, it is so rendered in his Arabic version: כלّ, *became wearied, exhausted*. However, Saadia himself calls attention to such an interchange on a few occasions. So in his comment on אגאלתי (Isa. 63.3) he states that it is like הגאלתי, with the *he* interchanged with an *alef*, as אֶתְחַבַּר (2 Chron. 20.35) = התחבר.[152] Also in his comment on וְהַוַת (Prov. 10.3) he observes that it may be rendered as וְאַוַת, with the *alef* interchanged with a *he*. In *Kitāb al-'Amānāt* (23, 1) he interprets ואל תרהו (Isa. 44.8) as ואל תיראו, "for in the art of permutation (פי צנאעה אלאבדאל) a *he* takes the place of an *alef*."[153]

---

[149] *Ibid.*, I, 18, 27 ff.

[150] *Ibid.*, II, 403, 18 ff. Also Menaḥem (*Maḥberet*, 75b) states with regard to the pleonastic *waw*: והוא'ו המוצב אשר לא מפעלו מפעל ואם נעדר מן המכתב לא נחסר העניין, citing a few examples, as ויכו (2 Sam. 14.6), וישנו (1 Sam. 21.14), למעינו (Ps. 114.8), etc.; see *Anfänge*, 88 ff.

[151] *Teshubot*, No. 98; see the rejoinder of Ibn Ezra, *Sefat Yeter*, No. 81.

[152] *Version arabe d'Isaie*, ed. Derenbourg, 142, 13 f.

[153] Similarly, in Part VII Saadia states that in אשכים (Jer. 25.3) and האדרש (Ezek. 14.3) the *he* is replaced by an *alef*, see p. 31 and n. 97, above; see also the fragment of the Introduction to his Commentary on the

Dunash mentions this part once more with reference to נחוץ (1 Sam. 21.9) which Saadia associates with לחוץ, for the *nun* interchanges with a *lamed*.[154] Again Saadia himself refers to this permutation. So in his comment on נטושה (Isa. 21.15) he states that he rendered it *polished* (=לטושה), for a *lamed* interchanges with a *nun*, as נשכה (Nehem. 13.6)=לשכה and נשכתו (ibid. 3.30) =לשכתו.[155] For the same reason Saadia renders ואלקום אללגט (Isa. 33.19)— ואת עם נועז, *the people speaking clamorously, an unintelligent language*, the same rendition he gives to לועז (Ps. 114.1). It is cited anonymously by Ibn Janāḥ, Ibn Bal‘am, Rashi, Ibn Ezra, Moses of England, and David Qimḥi, but viewed with disfavor by Ibn Janāḥ and rejected by Ibn Ezra with remark: והאומר כי הנון תחת הלמד לא דבר נכונה; however, Rashi states: נועז כמו לועז.[156] In his Introduction to the Agron Saadia employs the expression ישיחו נועז in the same meaning, too.[157]

Pentateuch, edited by Halkin, *Louis Ginzberg Jubilee Volume*, Hebrew Sec., 136, where a few other instances of such interchange are given.

[154] *Teshubot*, No. 115: ואמר בחילופין כי הנון תתחלף בלמד כדכתיב ... נחוץ כמות לחוץ (1 Sam. 21.9). Ibn Janāḥ (*Uṣūl*, 426, 10 ff.) cites this derivation with approval, then adds that it may also be a *nif‘al* of חוץ, as in ומי יחוש חוץ ממני (Eccl. 2.25), where חשתי<חוש=חוץ (Ps. 119.60), followed by Parḥon and Moses of England. Cf. *Maḥberet*, 93a, and *Sefat Yeter*, No. 88.

[155] *Version arabe d'Isaie*, 112, 5 ff. See Skoss, "A Chapter on Permutation in Hebrew" etc., *JQR*, N. S., XXIII, 15, n. 38.

[156] Their comm. on Isa. 33.19; see also Rashi on Ps. 114.1. Cf. *Mustalḥaq*, 37 f.

[157] Harkavy, *Zikron*, V, 54, 13; see n. 34, *ad loc.*, to which references should now be added also *Sefer ha-Shoham*, s. v. לעז. In his תפסיר אלסבעין לפטה, No. 84, Saadia associates לועז with ללועזות בלעז of the Talmud (Meg. 17a), criticized by Dunash (*Teshubot*, No. 45), who in turn associates it ומוציא לעז על בניו (Niddah, 13a). This derivation was first suggested by Ibn Qureish (*Risālah*, 42, 23 ff.) who cites another passage from the Talmud מוציא לעז על בניה (Qid. 81a), and followed by David b. Abraham (*Jāmi‘ al-Alfāẓ*, II, 172, 22 ff.), who equates לועז with the Arabic لغز and adds אללגז פי לגה אלערב טען ועיב ודם, "*laghz* means in the language of the Arabs *censure, reproach*, and *blame*." Ibn Qureish likewise renders it לאגז מפתרי, and Dunash: ופתרונה כמשמעה בלשון ערבי כמו משחית; see *Sefat Yeter*, No. 42.

Dunash likewise criticizes Saadia's identification of מזרות (Job 38.32) with מזלות (אלנגום)[158] and תאבתי (Ps. 119.174) with תאותי (אשתהית),[159] which most likely belong also to this part treating of permutation. The interchange of *lamed* and *resh* is likewise the reason for his association of גמר עלי (Ps. 57.3) with גמל נפשו (Prov. 11.17), both rendered אלמחסן, *who is beneficent*, similar to his rendition of יגמר בעדי (Ps. 138.8) — תפצל עלי, *he bestowed favor upon me*; also אלמנותיו (Isa. 13.22) is rendered by Saadia ארמנותיו = ארנקה. As for the permutation of *bet* and *waw*, Joseph Qimḥi quotes Saadia's opinion that גף (גפי Prov. 9.3), גב (גבי Ps. 129.3), and גו (Prov. 10.13) have the same signification, the *bet*, *waw*, and *pe* being homo-organic, they occasionally interchange with each other.[160] Indeed, all three are rendered by the Gaon טהר, *back*.

Other instances of permutation found in Saadia's works are in his comment on פזר (Ps. 112.9) that it is like בזר (ibid. 68.31), both meaning gifts (גואיז), for the *bet* interchanges with *pe*, as נשף (Isa. 40.24) = נשב (cf. ibid. 7), and ושופך (1 Chron. 19.16) = וישובך[161] (2 Sam. 10.16). The difficult verse חשקת נפשי משחת

David b. Abraham mentions several instances where the Hebrew ע = غ in Arabic.

[158] *Teshubot*, No. 84. Cf. *Maḥberet*, 83b; Ibn Ezra on Job 38.32 and *Sefat Yeter*, No. 72, and Qimḥi, *Shorashim*, s. v. It is cited anonymously in *Jāmiʿ al-Alfāẓ*, I, 506, 81 ff.; II, 195, 21 f., and rejected, but followed by Ibn Janāḥ (*Uṣūl*, 369, 24 ff.); Rashi; Comm. on Job 38.32 ascribed to Ibn Jiqaṭilla, ed. Bacher (אלברון), and Parḥon. It should be added, however, that already the Targum renders מזלא — מזרות.

[159] *Teshubot*, No. 96. Saadia's derivation is cited in *Jāmiʿ al-Alfāẓ*, II, 719, 18 f., and is followed by Yefet, Parḥon (*Maḥberet he-ʿAruk*, s. v.), and Qimḥi (*Shorashim*, s. v.). Menaḥem cites it from Ibn Qureish and rejects it (*Maḥberet*, 12b, 183b), giving to תאבתי and interpretation similar to that of Dunash; he is followed by Ibn Janāḥ (*Uṣūl*, 757, 5 ff.); Ibn Ezra on Ps. 119.174; J. Qimḥi (*Sefer ha-Galuy*, 161, 7 ff.), and Moses of England (*Sefer ha-Shoham*, s. v.).

[160] *Sefer ha-Galuy*, 8, 10 ff.; 79, 26 ff.

[161] *Saadja Al-fajjûmi's arab. Psalmenübers.*, ed. Lauterbach, XI, 15 ff., see editor's n. 7 on p. 36.

(Isa. 38.17) is rendered by him, צדדת נפסי מן אלהלאך, *Thou hast averted*, or *prevented*, *my soul from destruction*, as if it were חָשַׂכְתָּ,[162] with the interchange of *kaf* and *qof* and of *shin* and *sin*, cited anonymously by Ibn Bal'am, a rendition going back already to the LXX: ἀπόληται and the Vulgate: *eruisti*. Another instance of interchange of *sin* and *samekh* is Saadia's equation of וּשֵׂכָר (Prov. 26.10) with וַיִּסָּכְרוּ (Gen. 8.2), in the sense that the ignorant person withholds from others the little knowledge he possesses.[163] This comparison is cited by Rashi from Midrash Aggadah, but with a different interpretation. Dunash identifies ושכר with וסוגר, citing several instances of interchange of *sin* and *samekh*.[164] The permutation of *kaf* and *qof* is mentioned by Saadia in his תפסיר אלסבעין לפטה אלפרדה (Explanation of the Seventy Isolated Words), where יכרסמנה (Ps. 80.13) is equated with קרסמוה (Pe'ah 2, 7), as קובע[164a] = וכובע (1 Sam. 17.5) (ibid. 38). Moses of England compares הוברי שמים (Isa. 47.13) with וחובר חבר (Deut. 18.18), with the interchange of ע ח ה א, and on the margin is added וכן יסד רב סעדיה במחברתו.[165] However, in his Arabic version הוברי שמים is rendered מכתארו

---

[162] So, e. g., ולא חשכת ... ממני (Gen. 22.12) is rendered by Saadia, ולם תצד... עני.

[163] It is cited by Qimḥi, *Shorashim*, s. v. שכר. The same derivation is given by Saadia to כל־עשי שכר (Isa. 19.10).

[164] *Teshubot*, No. 79; the interchange of *kaf* and *gimel* is not mentioned, but perhaps וסוגר of the edited text should be read וסוכר. Cf. Comm. of Ibn Nachmias on Prov. 26.10 (ed. Bamberger, 151) for various interpretations of this difficult verse.

[164a] ר' סעדיה גאון, Jerusalem, 1943, 285, 9 ff., see Klar's note, *ad loc.*

[165] *Sefer ha-Shoham*, 64, 14 f., and n. 10. Menaḥem (*Maḥberet*, 12b), Ibn Bal'am, and J. Qimḥi (*Sefer ha-Galuy*, 66, s. v. אבחת) cite this derivation from Ibn Qureish and reject it. It is also criticized in *Jāmiʻ al-Alfāẓ*, I, 421, 55 ff., but approved by Ibn Janāḥ (*Uṣūl*, 169, 14 f.), Abraham ha-Babli (*JA*, 1863, II, 211), and Parḥon. Ibn Barūn (Kokowzoff, *Noviye Materiali*, 168ᵃ) and Qimḥi (*Shorashim*, s. v.) associate הברי with the Arabic هبر, *to cut*, since astrologers are people who decide matters; cf. חרטמין גזרין (Dan. 2.27).

היאֹה אלסמא, who choose an auspicious appearance of the skies, thus deriving it from ברר.

It is more than likely that many, if not all, of the above-mentioned instances were included in the part treating of permutation of Saadia's "Kutub al-Lughah", of which no fragments have been so far identified.[166]

It should be added here, however, that apart from Saadia's study of permutation three other similar studies of this subject were written in the X century. So we have the following statement of Judah ibn Qureish, a contemporary of the Gaon: "Whoever looks into our first book which is part *alef* . . ., will find in section *lamed* of that part a study of permutation of the letters of the whole alphabet, with proofs and examples drawn partly from the explanations of talmudic authorities and partly compiled from the entire Bible, clearly demonstrated."[167] Similarly Salmon b. Yeruḥam, a younger contemporary of Saadia and his bitter opponent, mentions in his Commentary on Lamentations several instances of permutation, especially of homo-organic consonants, referring to them as אחרף אלאבדאל, *letters of permutation*, then adds "I had written a separate book on these letters."[168] Unfortunately, these two treatises met with the same fate as Saadia's study, and they are no longer extant.

---

[166] For a study of Saadia's use of permutation in the interpretation of the biblical text see *JQR*, N. S., XXIII, 13 ff. In his comment on ביקרותיך (Ps. 45.10) Rashi cites ניקוד רב סעדיה, of which nothing is so far known. Bacher (*Anfänge*, 60, n. 2) suggests that it is perhaps to be identified with "Dagesh and Rafe," Part IV of "Kutub al-Lughah."

[167] Risālah, 43, 17 ff.: ומן נטֹר פי כתאבנא אלאול אלדֹי הו גֹזו אלף . . "יגד פי באב אללמד מן דֹלך אלגֹזו אבתדאל חרוף אלף בית כלהא בעצֹהא בבעץֹ באלדלאיל ואלשואהד מן שרח אהל אלתלמוד ומנהא מא אנתזעֹנאה מן גֹמיע אלמקרא בדלאיל ואצֹחהֹ.

[168] Feuerstein, *Commentar d. Karäers Salmon b. Jerucham z. d. Klageliedern*, XL, 29 ff.: וקד כנת עמלת להדֹה אלאאחרֹף כתאב מפרד; the edited text has erroneously עלמת, but see Munk, *Notice sur Abou'l-Walid*, 16, n. 1; 33, n. 1; 35, and 36, where this commentary is wrongly ascribed to Yefet; cf. Pinsker, *Liqquṭe Qad.*, Additions, 132.

However, the fourth study of permutation written in the second
half of the X century by David b. Abraham al-Fāsī and included
in his *Kitāb Jāmiʿ al-Alfāz* has come down to us. Since he had
most likely utilized at least some of the preceding treatises, his
study could probably be considered as a recapitulation or
summary of what has been done before him in this field.[169] At
any rate, most of the instances of interchange of consonants
cited by his three predecessors in their works are included in his
study, which gives us a pretty clear idea of permutation as
current in that formative period of Hebrew grammatical
studies.[170]

XI. Arabic Influence

There are some valid indications that Saadia was familiar
with Arabic grammatical usage and was influenced by it in his
studies of Hebrew grammar, as was already pointed out by
Bacher.[171] This is shown by the statements of the Gaon himself.

So in reference to עֲשִׂיתָנִי (Ezek. 29.3) in Part III, mentioned
above, he observed that "while the Arabs do say, 'I found
myself,' 'I taught myself,' thus joining the 1st. per. with the
objective suffix of the 1st per., the Hebrews have not sanctioned
such usage,"[172] etc. We have here then his comparison of
Arabic grammatical usage with that of Hebrew. Also in his

---

[169] See *Jāmiʿ al-Alfāz*, I, 439–445; the text of the Longer Version was
edited by the writer and published in *JQR*, N. S., XXIII, 1–13.

[170] Among later grammarians who made special studies of permutation
are Ibn Janāḥ (*Lumaʿ*, Chap. VI), Abraham ha-Babli (*JA*, 1863, II, 207 ff.),
Ibn Ezra (*Moznayim*, 12b f.), J. Qimḥi (*Zikkaron*, 71), and Profiat Duran
(*Maʿaseh Efod*, 81 ff.). For permutation in Arabic see *Sībawaihi*, ed.
Derenbourg, II, 340, 22 ff., and *Mufaṣṣal*², 172, 6 ff.

[171] *Anfänge*, 60 ff.

[172] *JQR*, N. S., XXXIII, 190, 6 ff.: וְעָלֵי אן אלערב יקולון וגדתוני עלّמתוני
פיזאוגّון אנא מע אנא פאן אלעבראניון לם יצטלחו עלי דֿלך אלך. See *Proceedings*,
XXI, 89 f. [15 f.].

Introduction to the *Agron* Saadia gives the following reason which impelled him to write it: "Just as the Arabs relate that one of their distinguished men, when he saw that some people do not speak the Arabic language correctly, he was grieved over it and composed a brief treatise from which they could learn correct speech, — I likewise saw a number of Israelites who do not observe the simplest rules of our language, not to mention the more difficult ones, and they mispronounce it in their speech . . . ., so I felt constrained to compose a book in which I shall compile most of the [Hebrew] words,"[173] etc. Furthermore, in the Commentary on *Sefer Yeṣirah*, in his remarks on the pronunciation of certain consonants, Saadia states that "a *jīm* is somewhere between a *gimel* and a *yod*, therefore the Tiberians pronounce it for a *yod* with a *dagesh*. Some Arabs substitute the *jīm* for a *yā*, for they say '*banū Alij*' meaning '*banū Aliyy*'," etc., then adds: "this is found in some grammars of the Arabic language."[174]

His Arabic designations which he occasionally employs in this Grammar for the Hebrew vowels likewise reflect this influence. So the *ḥolem* is termed (אלכביר) אלרפע אלאכבר, the *shureq* — (אלצגיר) אלרפע אלאצגר, the *qameṣ* — אלנצב אלאכבר, the *pataḥ* — אלנצב אלאוסט, the *segol* — (אלצגיר) אלנצב אלאצגר (also תֿלתֿ נקט), the *ḥireq* — אלכֿפֿץֿ אלאכבר (also just אלכֿפֿץֿ), and the *ṣere* — אלכֿפֿץֿ אלאצגר; but in two instances the last

---

[173] Harkavy, *Zikron*, V, 45, 3 ff.; וכמא ירוון בני אסמאעיל אן בעץ כואצֿהם ראי קומא לא יפצחון אלכלאם אלערבי פנמֿה דֿלך פוצֿע להם כלאמא מכתצרא פי כתאב יסתדֿלֹון בה עלי אלפציח כדֿלך ראית כתֿירא מן בני אסראיל לא יבצרון מרסל פציח לנתנא פכיף עויצה ואדֿא תכלמו כאן כתֿירא ממא ילפטֿון בה מלחונא . . . פאוגֿבת אן אוֿלף כתאבא אגֿמע פיה אכתֿר אללפטֿ אלך. See *Anfänge*, 60 ff.

[174] *Commentaire*, 43, 2 f. (Translation, 65): وهذا يوجد فى بعض كتب لغة العرب. See *Sībawaihi*, II, 342, 7 f.; *Mufaṣṣal²*, 176, 8 ff.; cf. also Rabin, *Ancient West Arabian*, 199 m.

term is employed to designate the *hireq*. This would indicate that Saadia takes the *holem*, *qameṣ*, and *hireq* as the three basic vowels.[175]

Yet, while this terminology may reflect some influence of Arabic grammar, Saadia's other grammatical terms only occasionally would indicate it. Thus, a definite noun is termed אלמערפה ;מקצוד, מתבת, or מחדוד, but rarely מערّף or an אלנכרה ;indefinite noun — מהמל or מטלק, but rarely מנכר or the construct state — אלנסבה, the absolute state — לדّאתה, a term used by Saadia also for the transitive and לגיר דّאתה for the intransitive verbs; the non-pausal form מוצّוע (also וצّע אלקול), and the pausal — מחמול, explained once אעני פּסוקה. The past tense is אלמאצّי, but the present — אלמקים and אלדאים, and the future — אלמסתקבל and אלאّתי, written frequently אלאיתי;[176] both אצל and ﻧוהר are used to designate

---

[175] Ibn Janāḥ (*Opuscules*, 275 f.) takes the *shureq, pataḥ*, and *hireq* as the three basic vowels, in accordance with the Arabic system, while according to Ibn Ezra (*Moznayim*, 8b; *Ṣaḥot*, 1a) they are the *holem, hireq*, and *pataḥ*. Cf. the classification of the Hebrew vowels by Judah ha-Levi (*al-Chazari*, ed. Hirschfeld, 130, 26 ff.): לאן נהאת אלנטק פי אלעבראניה באלקסמה תלתה צמה ופתחה וכסרה ובקסמה תّאניה צמה כברי והי קמץ ووסטי והי חולם וצגרי והי שורק ופתחה כברי והי פתח וצגרי והי סגל וכסרה כברי והי צירי וצגרי והי חירק, "For the vowel sounds are divided in Hebrew into three classes, viz., U-sound, A-sound, and I-sound, or in another divion: great U-sound ,or Qameṣ; medium U-sound, or *Ḥolem*; little U-sound, *Shureq*; great A-sound, or *Pataḥ*; little A-sound, or *Segol*; great I-sound, or *Ṣere*; little I-sound, or *Hireq*." (Hirschfeld's Translation, 129), but the last Arabic phrase is rendered by Ibn Tibbon: ושבר גדול והוא חירק וקטן והוא צרי. Thus, the three basic Hebrew vowels are, according to Judah ha-Levi, *qameṣ pataḥ*, and *ṣere* (or *hireq*); his statement likewise tends to indicate that he pronounced the *qameṣ* as an *o*-vowel, cf. Hirschfeld's n. 49 to his translation of this passage; see also *Ṣaḥot*, 3b, on the pronunciation of the *qameṣ*.

[176] The *yod* after an *alef* is occasionally used in Judeo-Arabic Mss. to designate the *medda*, see Derenbourg's Introduction to his edition of Saadia's Proverbs, XI; Goitein's edition of Abraham Maimonides, *Responsa*, XXVI, and Joel, *Siddur R. Saadia Gaon*, 56, 21. It is frequently used so in the Mss. of *Jāmiʻ al-Alfaẓ*, as ראיה = رآه (I, 260, 120; 288, 65); أجل = אלאיגל אינל,

a root or stem of a word; a vowel — נגמה (pl. נגם, נגמאת), instead of the usual חרכה. Occasionally a Hebrew term is arabicized, as דגש — דגשה, and its verb אדגש or אנדגש, to take a *dagesh*; קמץ — אלקאמצה or אלקמצה, and its verb מקמוץ (or יקמץ), having a *qames*; מכטוף, with *hatef*. Saadia uses frequently the Hebrew terms *dagesh* and *rafe*, but rarely the corresponding Arabic terms אלתשדיד ואלארכא.

This list of examples, incomplete as it is,[177] tends to show, I believe, that the Gaon was rather free and independent in the choice of his grammatical terminology. It may be of interest to note here that while he appears to have been familiar with Arabic grammar, he never employed the Arabic rule of إِدغام or اِدّغام, assimilation of one consonant to another, in his studies of Hebrew grammar,

XII. The Manuscripts

The Leningrad Ms. of "Kutub al-Lughah" was already briefly described in my preliminary report some twenty years ago,[178] but I believe that it should be described here in greater detail, as follows:

Hebrew-Arabic Ms. No. 3072, II Firkovitch Collection, 1st Series, 55 leaves, 17.5x13.5 cm., 21 lines to the page; clear Hebrew square characters with a tendency to cursiveness. As a rule diacritical points are found on the letters ﺝ=ج, ﻅ=ظ, and

الآجَل (*ibid.*, 539, 97, 99 nn.); אלאין=الآن (*ibid.*, II, 289, 10 n.). At times the *yod* is used to designate just a long *ā*, as ליכן=لكِنْ (*ibid.*, 130, 63 n., and elsewhere).

[177] Additional grammatical terms are to be found in Saadia's treatment of the particles and their functions, as אלכאף אלמתאליﹼﻪ, אלואו אלנסקיﹼﻪ, אלמים אלאקתבאסיﹼﻪ, etc., see above, p. 29, n. 103, and elsewhere.

[178] "Fragments of Unpublished Philological Works of Saadia Gaon," *JQR*, N. S., XXIII (1932–3), 329 ff., see 332.

צ̇ = ض, and occasionally, א = غ and ד = ذ. The Ms. is in good condition, though fols. 22, 23, 24, 25, 30, 31, 50, 51, and 53 are a little damaged with some loss of text. After the several misplaced leaves in the Ms. have been rearranged in consecutive order,[179] it was found to comprise fragments of the following parts and the number of leaves belonging to each part:

        II,   1a — 6b top;
       III,   6b — 21b;
        IV,   22b — 27a bottom;
         V,   27b — 33b;
        VI,   34a — 38a middle;
       VII,   38a — 49b top;
      VIII,   49b — 51b;
        IX,   52a — 55b.

As mentioned on previous occasions,[180] this Ms. was written by an ignorant or careless copyist, and it contains a number of scribal errors and some omissions. In my edition of the fragments of the various parts I have endeavored to correct these errors and to supply conjecturally the omissions in brackets like these < >, but I am far from certain that I have always succeeded in this task.

The four small fragments of "Kutub al-Lughah," recently identified at Oxford and Cambridge, are as follows:

1. Bodleian Library at Oxford, No. 2835 (Ms. Heb. c. 27), fol. 73, 22¼ cm. square. It is an old vellum leaf with most of the left side and both lower corners torn off, with loss of text. It is

---

[179] In view of the circumstance that Saadia occasionally treats the same grammatical points in various parts, as, e. g., the vocalization of prefixes and particles are treated in Part IV (Dagesh and Rafe) and also in Part VII (Laryngeals and non-Laryngeals), it is at times difficult to identify some single leaves to which part they may belong. So I am not quite certain that I have placed each fragment in the part to which it really belongs.

[180] *JQR*, N. S., XXXIII, 173; XLII, 289.

very closely written, containing 59 lines on the recto and 64 lines on the verso; the writing, very small old beautiful Hebrew square, is badly rubbed off, so that it could be read in places only with the aid of an ultra-violet lamp.[180a]

The first 19 lines of the recto contain the end of another work by Saadia Gaon, evidently treating of the controversial subject that knowledge of the principles of the revealed law and its ramifications could be acquired only by way of study of the tradition (פַֿאד קד אוצחת אן אלוצול אלי אצול אלשרע אלסמעי וﬠרוﬠה לא יכון אלא בטריק אלנקל אלך). most likely arguing against Analogy (אלקיאס[181]). Saadia refers here also to his "Kitāb al-Tamyīz" (כמא ביננא פי כתאב אלתמייז). It ends with כמלת אלמקאלה אלב והי אכר אלכתאב בﬠון אלרחמן תﬦ אלכתאב ולאלה (so) אלחמד.

Then follows on a separate line בשם רחמנא ברכה משוכה, after which begins the text of Part III of "Kutub al-Lughah," with many variants and more correct than that of the Leningrad Ms., edited by me and published in *JQR*, N. S., 174 ff. The closely written fragment covers almost two-thirds of the edited text, to ibid., 196, 1. 10 לבﬠץ.

2. Taylor-Schechter Genizah Collection at Cambridge, Box K-7, 19. It belongs to the same Ms. as the preceding fragment, its text being a continuation of the latter. But this vellum leaf is much more damaged than the other, with the left side and lower portion torn off, its present size being only 16.5 x 13 cm. It resumes in the edited text just about two lines after the text of

---

[180a] In Neubauer-Cowley's *Catalogue of Hebrew Mss.*, II, 275, this fragment is marked as "Fragment of a theological work in Arabic; a section beg. בשם . . . אלגז אלג מן אליב אלגזו אלך; but this is the beginning of the first paragraph of Part III of "Kutub al-Lughah," as edited by me, see *JQR*, N. S., XXX, 174, 1 (*Saadia Studies*, 66, 1).

[181] The fragment probably belongs to Saadia's work כתאב דפﬠ אלקיאס פי אלפראיץ א לסמﬠיה, previously mentioned in this study, see *Proceedings*, XXI, 98, [24].

the Bodleian fragment breaks off, but with many lacunae as a result of the torn parts, and its text extends to about a page more than that of the Leningrad fragment edited by me.[182]

3. T.-S. Collection at Cambridge, Arabic 32, 29, 1 paper leaf, about one third torn off lengthwise from the right, but otherwise well preserved; at present 22 x 11 cm., 18 lines to the page, written in large Hebrew square. It contains a portion of Part III, beginning in the edited text with ibid., 184, l. 8 ועלי, and ending on p. 186, l. 8, with אלכמס מעארף (Ms. . . . אלה מצא).

4. T.-S. Collection at Cambridge, Arabic 31, 247, 4 paper leaves, badly damaged and torn and the lower portion torn off; originally 28 x 18 cm. and 45–6 lines to the page, but now its height is only about 18–19 cm. The writing, very small, somewhat cursive Hebrew square, is in places so rubbed off that it could not be deciphered even with the aid of an ultra-violet lamp. Its contents were previously described at some length,[183] so there is no need dwelling upon it here again, except that of "Kutub al-Lughah" it embraces the end of Part III and probably the entire Part IV, though with a great many lacunae due to torn parts. But its text presents a different version from that of the Leningrad Ms.

XIII. Conclusion

The foregoing rather brief survey of all the so far available manuscript material of Saadia Gaon's "Kutub al-Lughah," the earliest Hebrew grammar extant, fragmentary as it is, unfolds

---

[182] This fragment was identified in summer, 1947, by my friend Dr. Nehemiah Allony, from Jerusalem, who was kind enough to send me photostats of it. I am deeply indebted to him for his kindness, as well as for his ever ready assistance during my stay in England the following summer, when I was fortunate enough to identify the other three fragments belonging to Saadia's Grammar.

[183] See *Proceedings*, XXI, 91 [17], 97 f. [23 f.].

before our eyes a fair enough picture of the beginnings of this science. We are witnessing here its first faltering and uncertain steps before the earliest distinction between strong and weak verbs was made by Dunash b. Labraṭ,[184] leading to the tri-consonantal theory of Hebrew stems, the scientific principles of which were definitely established by Judah Ḥayyūj at the end of the X and the beginning of the XI centuries.

Saadia's grammatical views appear to present the first post-masoretic stage in the development of Hebrew grammar. In this earliest attempt at independent study of this science he was greatly influenced by the Masorah, whose primary aim was the preservation of the biblical text as transmitted by tradition, with its occasional irregularities and deviations from the accepted usage, including its vocalization and accentuation. The con-sonantal as well as the vocalic make-up of some grammatical forms was taken as accepted by usage, without trying to discover any particular reason for it. So Saadia groups, e. g., the verbal forms שִׁבֵּר, הִצִּיל, and הִכָּה together, because all three have a *dagesh* in the middle radical and their participial forms begin with a preformative *mem*, without any attempt at identifying the different stems of these forms.

The second stage in the development of Hebrew grammatical theory is presented in the lexical works of Menaḥem b. Saruq and the Karaite David b. Abraham al-Fāsī. They recognize as radicals only those consonants which are present in the various inflections of a given stem, disregarding the consonants which are omitted in some of its formations. This brought them to the theory of Hebrew stems, consisting of one, two, three, and more consonants, as, e. g., כ is the stem of הכה (ויך), צל is the stem of הציל (יציל), etc.[185]

---

184 See n. 187, below.
185 *Maḥberet*, 39b ff.; *Jāmi' al-Alfāẓ*, I, 4, 92 ff., Introduction, lxviii ff. Of

The views of Dunash b. Labraṭ may be taken as representing the third stage in the development of Hebrew grammar. At first, in his criticism of Menaḥem, he, too, recognized uni-consonantal and bi-consonantal stems, only to a much more limited degree than the two above-mentioned authorities.[186] But later, in his critical notes on Saadia, he makes reference to strong and weak verbs;[187] he may be, therefore, considered the first to allude to the tri-consonantal theory of Hebrew stems. Accordingly, his views could be regarded as representing the transition period from the views of Menaḥem and David b. Abraham to the scientifically developed tri-consonantal theory of Ḥayyūj.[188] Thus could be briefly outlined the three stages in the development of

uni-consonantal stems Menaḥem counts nineteen, viz. מ ל כ ט ח ז ה ה ד ג ב ת ש ר ק צ פ ע ס ן, see *Maḥberet*, 40a ff., where several examples for each of these are cited. On the other hand, David b. Abraham enumerates only fourteen uni-consonantal stems, omitting from Menaḥem's list the consonants ע, מ ל ח ב, see *Jāmiʿ al-Alfāẓ*, I, 5, 113 ff., Introduction,ʹ lxix ff. (cf. also *ibid.*, II, cxxxix, addition to lxix, n. 94, l. 5).

[186] Dunash refers only to five uni-consonantal stems, viz. ג (וַיַּגֶּה, Lam. 3.33), ד (וַיַּדּוּ, *ibid.* 53), ז (יְזֶה, Lev. 6.20), ט (יִטֶּה, Job 15.29), and כ (יֻכָּה, Ex. 21.20); see *Teshubot* against Menaḥem, 23, 26, 27, 55; cf. also Yellin, תולדות התפתחות הדקדוק העברי, Jerusalem, 1945, 74.

[187] Dunash refers to the strong verb as שלם and to the weak מסוכן or מסתכן (the Arabic صحيح and معتلّ, respectively). So *Teshubot* against Saadia, No. 21, on זבדני (Gen. 30.20): והחריב מלה משולשת שלימה ועשאה התבונן ואל תתעלם מן המעשים המסוכנות בפה, and No. 36: מסוכנת כמו זבת ובעין ובלמד שלהן; see also Nos. 46, 51, 56, 101, 110. In this connection it is of special interest to quote here the significant statement of Ibn Ezra in *Safah Berurah*, 25b: דע כי כל הקדמונים היו אומרים כי שרש ירד רד לבדו, ושרש ישב ככה, ושרש עשה עש לבדו, וככה ימצאו ברבי הפיוטים הקדמונים, ושרש נגע נע ושרש נטה טי״ת לבדו, ויז על אהרן (ויקרא ח' ל') זי״ן לבדו, ושרש מכה אביו (שמות כ״א ט״ו) כ״ף לבדו. זאת היתה דעת ר' יהודה בן קריש ור' מנחם בן סרוק, רק ר' אדונים הלוי הקיץ מעט משנת האולת, כי הנזכרים תרדמת השם נפלה עליהם, ויפקח אלהים את עיני ר' יהודה ב״ר דוד הנקרא חיוג להכיר אותיות הנוח ואיך הם נוספים ונעדרים ומתחלפים. See *Anfänge*, 101 ff., and *Jāmiʿ al-Alfāẓ*, 1, Introduction, lxxxvi and n. 127.

[188] The rejoinder of Menaḥem's disciples (תשובות תלמידי מנחם) does not add anything to the study of Hebrew stems. For a study of this work see Yellin *op. cit.*, 94 ff.

Hebrew grammatical theory from the masorete Aaron b. Asher, in the beginning of the X century, to Judah Ḥayyūj, at the end of that century.

However, it was Saadia Gaon who laid the foundation of the scientific treatment of Hebrew grammar, and his contributions in this field can hardly be overestimated. Unfortunately, the direct influence of his "Kutub al-Lughah" on later grammarians was rather short-lived.[189] For already in the first half of the XI century Ibn Janāḥ cites this Grammar from Saadia's quotations from it in his Commentary on *Sefer Yeṣirah*, then adds that he never saw it nor did it get to Spain.[190] Similarly Abraham ibn Ezra evidently knew of it only from the critical remarks of Dunash, to which he wrote the rejoinder שפת יתר, as mentioned in the beginning of this study.[191] Also Profiat Duran, who very likely got his information from Ibn Ezra, states that Saadia wrote three grammatical works which "did not reach us."[192]

[189] For Saadia's influence on Ḥayyūj see above, 28, n. 88.

[190] See *ibid*.

[191] *Proceedings*, XXI, 76 [2].

[192] *Ma'aseh Efod*, 44: והיה מי שהתעורר ראשונה והתחיל לכתוב בחכמה הזאת הגאון רבינו סעדיה שנסמך לגאונות בשנת ארבעה אלפים ת״ר פ״ז ליצירה חבר בה שלשה ספרים לא הגיעו אלינו.